HOW TO LIVE AND

In this Series

How to Be a Local Councillor
How to Be an Effective School
  Governor
How to Buy & Run a Shop
How to Buy & Run a Small Hotel
How to Choose a Private School
How to Claim State Benefits
How to Conduct Staff Appraisals
How to Do Your Own Advertising
How to Employ & Manage Staff
How to Enjoy Retirement
How to Get a Job Abroad
How to Get a Job in America
How to Get a Job in Australia
How to Get a Job in Europe
How to Get an American Visa
How to Get That Job
How to Help Your Child at School
How to Invest in Stocks & Shares
How to Keep Business Accounts
How to Know Your Rights at Work
How to Know Your Rights: Patients
How to Know Your Rights: Students
How to Know Your Rights: Teachers
How to Live & Work in America
How to Live & Work in Australia
How to Live & Work in Belgium
How to Live & Work in France
How to Live & Work in Germany
How to Live & Work in Hong Kong

How to Live & Work in Japan
How to Live & Work in Saudi Arabia
How to Live & Work in Spain
How to Lose Weight & Keep Fit
How to Make It in Films & TV
How to Manage People at Work
How to Master Book-keeping
How to Master Business English
How to Master GCSE Accounts
How to Master Public Speaking
How to Pass Exams Without Anxiety
How to Pass That Interview
How to Plan a Wedding
How to Prepare Your Child for School
How to Publish a Newsletter
How to Raise Business Finance
How to Raise Funds & Sponsorship
How to Run a Local Campaign
How to Spend a Year Abroad
How to Start a Business from Home
How to Study Abroad
How to Study & Live in Britain
How to Survive at College
How to Survive Divorce
How to Take Care of Your Heart
How to Teach Abroad
How to Use a Library
How to Write a Report
How to Write for Publication
How to Write for Television

LIVE & WORK IN JAPAN

A practical guide for expatriates

Aaron Hoopes

How To Books

British Library cataloguing-in-publication data
A catalogue record for this book is available
from the British Library.

© 1992 by Intercultural Press

First published in 1992 by How To Books Ltd, Plymbridge House, Estover
Road, Plymouth PL6 7PZ, United Kingdom. Tel: Plymouth (0752)
735251/695745 Fax: (0752) 695699. Telex: 45635.

Typeset by Concept Communications Ltd, Crayford, Kent.
Printed and bound in Great Britain by
Dotesios Ltd, Trowbridge, Wiltshire.

Contents

1   Introducing Japan   9

    Geography and people   9
    The climate of Japan   11
    History and government   11
    The economy   15

2   Before you leave   19

    Visas   19
    Entry regulations and restrictions   20
    Pets   21
    Clothing   21

3   Arriving in Japan   25

    Transport   25
    Money matters   29
    Immigration regulations   31
    Street addresses   33
    Keeping in touch   33
    Security   36
    Resources for visitors   40

4   Coping with the language   41

    Meanings and nuances   41
    Writing   43
    Pronunciation   44
    Learning Japanese   46
    Language schools   46

5   Coping with the culture   49

    Religions and philosopies   50
    Harmonious relationships   52
    Communication   56
    Customs and courtesies   58

6 Doing business in Japan   63

   The Japanese business relationship   63
   Inside a Japanese company   65
   Contracts, the law and tradition   70
   How to use interpreters   72
   Business customs   72
   Business mechanics   75
   Business hotels   76
   Visiting Japanese companies   77

7 Daily living for expats   78

   Housing   78
   Furnishings, appliances and electricity   80
   Telephones   81
   Domestic help   81
   Shopping   82
   Role of a non-working spouse   84
   Foreign residents advisory centres   85

8 Health and medical care   86

   Public health   86
   Medical care   86
   Clinics and hospitals   87
   Dental care   89
   Emergency services   89
   Councelling services   90
   Health insurance   90
   Pharamacies   90

9 Schools   92

   The Japanese education system   92
   Entering the Japanese system   93
   International schools   94
   Preschool children   95
   School addresses   95
   International colleges and universities   98
   Educational information   99

10 Cars and driving   100

   Congestion and delays   100
   Buying and maintaining a car   100
   Driving licences   101

11 Japan at leisure   103

      Eating and drinking   103
      The arts   107
      Music, theatre and films   108
      Living national treasures   109
      Diversions   109
      Sports   110
      Festivals   113
      Travel in Japan   113

12 The major cities   117

      Tokyo   117
      Kyoto   121
      Osaka   126
      Kobe   131

Japanese glossary   133
Useful addresses   141
Further reading   149
Index   153

List of illustrations

1   Japan and its neighbours   8

2   Japan by road and rail   38–39

3   Tokyo   118

4   Kyoto   124

5   Osaka   128

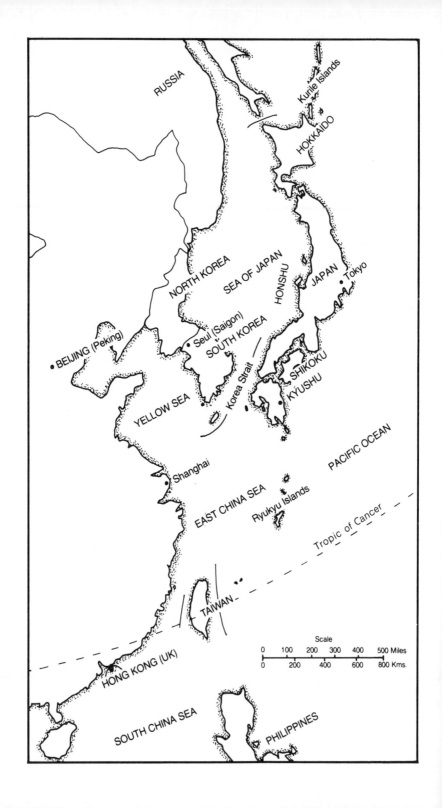

1
Introducing Japan

It was believed in ancient times that Japan was the eastern-most land of the world and the closest to the realm of the sun which rose from the sea each day. According to the ancient myths of the indigenous religion, Shinto, the Japanese are descendants of deities, and the emperor is the god on earth whose lineage stretches back to the sun goddess herself. The two characters which the Japanese have used to symbolise their country are the ideographs of the sun and of rising.

The Land of the Rising Sun is also a land of contrasts and, according to some, paradoxes. Japan is struggling to integrate the traditional and the modern and to continue the transition from a past founded on agriculture to a future based on technology. Exploration of Japan's history, its geography, and its people will provide intriguing insights into this remarkable society and its current worldview. And there is much for the newcomer to learn.

GEOGRAPHY AND PEOPLE

A country of volcanic islands

Modern Japan is made up of the four large islands of Hokkaido, Honshu, Kyushu, and Shikoku, and over four thousand smaller ones. Japan's total land area is 145, 856 square miles, comparable to the state of California and similarly situated on the Circum-Pacific earthquake zone. Three-quarters of Japan's population of over 123 million live on the main island of Honshu; one-third of these live in and around Tokyo, the world's second most populous city.

The islands' volcanic origins have produced magnificent mountains, which make up 80 percent of Japan's total land area. Since this land is unsuitable for farming or urban development, the remaining 20 percent must support a population half that of the United States, which makes it one of the most densely populated countries in the world. In some areas the population density is three times that of New York City.

9

Even though Japan is not agriculturally self-sufficient, it has the distinction of producing more food per acre than any other country in the world; farmers cultivate every available open space. Since feeding and keeping livestock in such crowded conditions is not economical, Japan has directed its energy to the sea, supporting the world's largest fishing fleet — nearly half a million boats. Understandably, fish replaces meat in most diets, and meat prices can seem staggeringly high. Poor in minerals and natural resources, Japan must import much of the raw material it needs — oil, iron, ore, cotton, wool, timber, and coal.

The people of Japan
Of the 123 million people living in Japan today, an overwhelming majority are descendants of families that have lived in the archipelago for centuries. Japan is notable for its lack of ethnic diversity. Such marked homogeneity can lead to severe problems for those considered different.

The two minority groups most evident in Japan are Koreans, who make up approximately six percent of the population, and the extremely controversial **Burakumin**. A third minority group which has not yet gained as much publicity is the **Ainu**, an indigenous Caucasoid population which over the centuries has been pushed to the northernmost areas of the archipelago.

The Koreans
Many of the Koreans who live in Japan today are descendants of the large numbers who were forced to migrate to Japan as labourers after the occupation of Korea in 1910. Historically the Koreans and the Japanese have been fierce rivals. Korea has been depicted as a dagger pointed at the heart of Japan and responses to this perceived threat find their outlet in Japan in both legal and social discrimination. For instance, individuals of Korean descent whose families have lived in Japan for generations must continue to register as aliens, year after year, and a 1948 law persists which bars Koreans from becoming school teachers in the public sector.

The Burakumin
The other minority group we have mentioned are the Burakumin. Between the sixteenth and nineteenth centuries, a caste system developed which placed the warriors at the top, followed by farmers, craft workers and merchants, in that order. At the very bottom of the heap were the Burakumin, the equivalent of the outcasts of the Hindu caste system.

The current estimated population of the Burakumin is about three million. Extremely strong prejudices against this group remain and, though often denied by those in public office, underlying oppressive attitudes persist. As recently as the early seventies books were published with biographical data on all the Burakumin families so that people could make sure that potential family members were not of this group.

Educational and economical disadvantages persist for the Burakumin and an extremely high proportion do not even finish school. Since one must have a high school degree to get a job in a factory or work as a civil servant, and one cannot afford to send one's children to good schools unless one has a good job, the Burakumin are trapped in a vicious circle of economic and educational deprivation.

THE CLIMATE OF JAPAN

Most of Japan has four distinct seasons, although their length and intensity vary according to latitude. In Tokyo and other districts of central Honshu the temperature averages about 14°C but goes below freezing in winter and into the mid 30°Cs in summer. Tokyo is very humid, and, while it may not seem so cold by the thermometer, the dampness is chilling in winter. The coldest month is February, the hottest is August. It rains about twice as much in Tokyo as in London, with June being the rainiest month. Summer is damp and hot, autumn is pleasantly cool and relatively dry, while winter is generally cold with bright sunshine.

Snowfall occurs most in the mountains and in the north. There are many ski areas in the mountains of Honshu, which are to the west and within easy reach of Tokyo. Hokkaido in the north has a much colder climate, with at least five months of snow a year providing excellent skiing. Kyushu, to the south, is far more temperate; just right for growing oranges.

Spring arrives in April, with cherry blossoms appearing early in the month. Cherry blossom time is a festive period in Japan; nearly everyone turns out to enjoy the glorious flowering trees. Spring outings under the cherry blossoms are a ritual, and the settings in which they can be viewed range from tiny gardens near private homes to a valley near Kyoto, where 100,000 trees may be seen from Arashi Mountain.

HISTORY AND GOVERNMENT

Over the centuries, isolationist policies have allowed Japan to develop at its own pace with a minimum of outside interference. Modern Japanese society is firmly rooted in a long and rich past. If a visitor to the country of today is to appreciate the land and its people, a general understanding of the Japan of yesterday is vital. Toward this end we present a thumbnail sketch of Japan's past.

Ancient history

Japan's history stretches back more than ten thousand years to Neolithic times. During the **Yayoi** period, from about the third century BC to the third century AD, the Japanese laid the foundation for today's society by mastering the cultivation of rice. Many Japanese values and forms of behaviour, especially concerning cooperation and the avoidance of conflict, stem from the culture which developed around the rice growing economy.

During the Yayoi period powerful warlords began to consolidate the hundreds of states that existed throughout the islands. One ruling family in the Kansei area of southern Honshu managed eventually to bring the whole of Japan together under its control. According to ancient texts, the found of this family was Emperor Jinmu, who began his reign in the year 660 BC. Members of today's ruling family are said to be direct descendants of this first emperor. Jinmu's date of ascension, February 11, has been marked as Japan's National Foundation Day.

The Middle Ages

From the fourth to the twelfth centuries the emperor rules in conjunction with powerful landholding families. Extensive contact with the civilisations of China and Korea from the third to the seventh century AD had an enormous impact on Japanese culture. During that period Buddhism, the Chinese ideographic writing system and court manners and style of dress were adopted by the Japanese emperor and his entourage. New ideas concerning architectural styles and city planning as well as artistic trends and techniques practised by crafts workers also found fertile ground in the archipelago.

In the centuries which followed, the Japanese experienced a 'golden age' as the Chinese influence was absorbed into Japanese culture. The arts flourished, temples and shrines were built, cities grew.

Politics in Japan have alternated between periods in which imperial rule weakened and feudal clans led by warrior generals vied for power. Eventually the **Samurai** warriors who were hired by noble landholders to keep the rice growing peasants under control, gained enough power to claim almost absolute control of the country.

In the late sixteenth century, the entire country and all of its warrior factions were unified by the warlord Hideyoshi Toyotomi. During this era the great Osaka castle was built and the invasions of Korea and China were launched. Upon Toyotomi's death, his successor, Teyasu Tokugawa took the title of Shogun and moved the capital from Kyoto to the eastern city of Edo, which ultimately became the Tokyo of today. Before Tokugawa, the title of Shogun had been given to the general in charge of fighting barbarian tribes in the north. It now, however, came to stand for the warrior lord who held the reins of the entire Japanese government. For three hundred years the Tokugawa Shogunate was the predominant controlling force in Japan.

In 1543 the first Westerners arrived in Japan from Portugal. For a brief time the Japanese tolerated contact as traders and missionaries sought to open up new markets for goods and to introduce Christianity. In the early seventeenth century, however, the Shogunate abruptly broke off all relations with the outside world. It closed the country to all foreign commerce except for tightly controlled trading with protestant Dutch through the port of Nagasaki. Thus the perpetuation of what was then a flourishing feudal society of the nobility, peasants, and professional soldiers (samurai) was assured.

Modern times

Japan remained closed to outsiders until 1854, when Commodore Matthew Perry sailed into Tokyo Bay with his black warships and demanded that Japan participate in foreign trade. This event allowed groups dissatisfied with the Tokugawa Shogunate to gain enough power to reinstate the Emperor Meiji as the active head of state, thus ending the Shogunate's three-century rule.

Under the guidance of the Emperor Meiji, the country embarked on a course of rapid economic growth and industrial development which soon brought Japan into the modern world. Japan's government was established as a constitutional monarchy composed of separate judicial and legislative branches, with the emperor as head of state. The army and navy were remodelled after their German and British counterparts, and a period of exchange began between Japan and Western nations which rapidly allowed Japan to gain the knowledge and skills necessary to catapult itself into the twentieth century. The wisely managed domestic growth of the Meiji period laid the foundation for the superpower which Japan has become in recent years.

With the advent of the Great Depression in 1929, militaristic factions in the government gained greater control and were able to influence domestic and international policy to an increasing extent. These groups masterminded the aggressive expansionism that climaxed in the Second World War.

The government of Japan today

After World War Two (1939-45) Japan had to rebuild virtually from scratch. With the start of the American Occupation, the government was changed to a constitutional democracy with the emperor serving merely as a figurehead.

Looking at Japanese politics from the outside, one may get the mistaken impression of similarity to that of Western democracies. It has universal suffrage and secret ballots for elective offices. The executive branch is responsible to the Diet (Parliament) which consists of two houses, the House of Representatives (which is the more powerful) and the House of Councillors. Executive power is vested in a cabinet (the prime minister and ministers of state), and the judicial system is based on Roman law with several levels of courts and a supreme court that exercises final authority. Changes in political leadership occur without violence.

Despite these similarities, however, the political process in Japan is very different from that of the West. It is characterised more by consensus building, than by executive and legislative leadership. Politicians and political parties do not lead; they wait to see how compromise will be worked out between different traditional factions. Major decisions in politics, as in business, are generally made only after lengthy consideration at all levels of the bureaucracy. Charismatic leadership is not valued in Japan as it is in the West.

Currently five parties compete for the spotlight in Japanese politics. These are the:

Liberal Democratic party (LDP)
Japan Socialist party (JSP)
Democratic Socialist party (DSP)
Komeito (Clean Government Party)
Japanese Communist party (JCP).

From its founding in 1955 until 1989 the moderately conservative Liberal Democratic Party dominated Japanese politics. But the LDP was weakened by the Recruit Scandal in early 1989, in which many LDP members were caught accepting large amounts of preflotation stock, and the hasty implementation of the badly flawed consumption tax passed the year before. The result was a loss of the party's absolute majority in the ensuing election and the emergence of the Socialist party as a stronger political force. Only time can tell whether the conservative LDP, which gave Japan the stability it needed to recover from a defeated and war torn state, will be able to lead the country into the new challenges of the twenty-first century.

The Emperor

Until the end of World War Two the emperor was regarded as divine and was treated as a living god; common people were forbidden to look upon him. After Japan's defeat the emperor was officially designated a mortal. Emperor Hirohito, whose 64-year reign (1925 to 1989) was called the **Showa Era**, was the longest reigning emperor in Japanese history. Hirohito was succeeded by his son, Akihito, whose reign is called the **Heisei Era**.

Akihito was born in 1933 and is the first member of the imperial family to be raised more or less as an ordinary child. In 1959 he married Michiko Shada, the daughter of an important businessman with no imperial ties. Akihito's 'imperial style' differs considerably from his father's as he attempts to make greater contact with the Japanese people. Despite the changes in recent decades, the imperial family still plays a prominent role in Japanese society.

THE ECONOMY

The people of Japan possess a native talent for adapting and improvising and a deep sense of thrift; they tend towards saving and reinvestment and are committed to hard work. The result is well known by business people the world over. Despite its lack of raw materials Japan is one of the major industrial producers of the world. The Japanese are taking great chunks of the market in Europe and North America in synthetic fibres, electronics, cameras, cars, trucks, and many other products. They are steadily winning massive contracts throughout the Middle East and have signed long-range and extensive trade agreements with the People's Republic of China.

Influences of the past

As mentioned above, ancient Japanese culture developed around a rice growing economy. For hundreds of years the structure of Japanese society involved three tiers: the noble landholding families, the Samurai warrior class, and the rice-growing peasants. During the Tokugawa Shogunate, the warrior class became the most powerful element of the society and controller of the economy. Another group, the merchant class, also gained strength during the centuries of peaceful commerce. With the Meiji Restoration the elite families who controlled the economy were naturally the ones with the wealth and power to lead the industrialisation of Japan. They shifted gears and assumed their new role as business conglomerates with ease.

During World War Two the Japanese economy was largely destroyed.

The industries that survived were antiquated and had a reputation for producing inferior goods. The great business 'families' which dominated the industrialisation of the country before proved to be virtually impossible to break up. When banned and scattered by Occupation legislation, they merely formed again when the Americans formally left in 1952. Today's incarnation of the iron-clad family networks of old are the great trading companies whose influence reaches to all corners of the economy.

Factors for growth

A combination of critical factors has helped Japan's rapid economic development: sophisticated industrial and economic policies; highly developed skills in maths, science, and applied technology; a disciplined and dedicated workforce capable of high productivity; a powerful group outlook and readiness for personal sacrifice; and strong capabilities in business organisation, management, and strategic planning. All these factors have proved to be a recipe for success in the global marketplace.

In most free countries economic progress involves negotiation, competition, and often conflicts among banks, business, and government. In Japan all three institutions appear to work together like an army staff at the company level, a system that has led Japan to receiving the nickname 'Japan, Inc.' This conforms to the Japanese preference for harmony in overt social interactions. Below the surface, however, Japanese business executives are in some ways fiercely competitive. Gaining market share over competitors both at home and abroad is a principal goal of major Japanese corporations, and they will even sacrifice their subsidiaries toward this end.

Japan is committed to commercial and industrial growth, not simply by governmental or business policy but as a national objective very much linked to the country's survival. This commitment is inculcated in Japanese youngsters at an early age. It is taught in school and reinforced through the group orientation of the culture and by the economic forces with which the country contends. It is supported by the family-like structure of business, where the loyalty of employees is matched by the company's lifetime commitment to the care of and concern for them. Finally, it is embodied in the intricate relationship between government and industry. The Ministry of International Trade and Industry (MITI) works very closely with Japanese businesses in both planning economic policies and carrying them out.

Trading companies

Trading companies, called **shosha**, for all practical purposes control the country's international trade. The word denotes a marketing organisation that not only participates in several types of manufacturing on an equity basis but at the same time acts as a wholesale distributor of the products. One trading company will frequently have a direct interest in both the wholesale and retail operations and will act as an exporter, often owning its own ships. It will also often import for distribution and may supply the manufacturer with raw materials.

'Mr Company President' is modern Japan's equivalent to its classical authority figure, the feudal lord. As the head of a major manufacturing company, he is backed by an army of support institutions, or **keiretsu**, and an infantry of second-tier companies that serve to provide the raw materials, subcontracting skills, and support functions required for the maintenance of an economic giant. In this way, the small to middle-sized manufacturer, who always seems short of working capital, may have access to an in-house banker, exporter, importer, purchasing agent, and local marketing agent.

Although there are over five thousand trading companies in Japan, ten handle 50 percent of Japan's exports and 60 percent of its imports. Mitsubishi and Mitsui each handle 10 percent or more of the import-export market, followed by Marubeni, Itochu, Nissho-Iwai, and Sumitomo.

One should not, however, make the mistake of thinking of Japan only in terms of manufacturing giants like these, or of Sony, Toyota, and Honda. One of the great strengths of this least understood world power lies in its small or medium-sized firms. In fact, of the nearly five million individual enterprises listed in Japan, more than 98 percent are classified as small or medium, which means employing fewer than three hundred people, These small establishments account for over twenty-seven million employees, more than half the workforce of the nation. They are the backbone of the country's economy and form a chain of subcontractors that provide the millions of parts the giant companies must have to circle the earth with their goods.

Recent trends

In 1989, exports amounted to over $269 billion, and Japan's GNP was $2.836 trillion, yielding a per capita GNP of $23,040. Such figures put Japan high on the list of wealthiest nations in the world. Japan has risen to industrial and commercial preeminence and has become a leading, if not *the* leading, producer of electronic products, cars, steel, shipping, and high-tech consumer goods. Even with the import of most of its raw materials, Japan's export growth has strongly outstripped imports and has resulted in a large annual trade surplus and accumulation of foreign exchange reserves. For investors the Tokyo Stock Exchange is one of the most attractive and lucrative outside the US and Europe (though there have been steep falls in prices over the last two years).

The US is and will probably continue to be Japan's largest trading partner, making up about one-third of Japan's world market and providing one fifth of each year's imports according to 1989 US State Department figures. In future years Americans in particular can be expected to take increasingly stronger positions on trade restrictions and to push their own industries to match Japanese organisational and technical accomplishments. If their efforts are to be successful they will have to provide the training that business executives need to be more effective in cross-cultural operations.

In recent years Japan's 'economic miracle' has shown evidence of plateauing. The growth rate of the GNP has begun to fall slowly, and unemployment figures have begun to rise. It is very difficult to forecast the future of Japan because figures can be misleading. Unemployment figures, for instance, do not necessarily mean lack of opportunity. A major problem in Japan today is that there are actually more jobs than applicants. This labour shortage is seen by some to be indicative of a shift in worker attitudes. Individuals have become more choosy about what jobs they will take, and young people are more likely to adopt 'a work a little, play a little' mentality. Rather than taking menial jobs as careers, they may work long hours for high wages over a limited period of time and then 'take a break', knowing that because of the labour shortage they will have no difficulty in finding employment later.

Whatever the case, Japan remains a key player in global economics. Major Japanese companies are among the largest in the world, and their operations are ever more international in nature. Japan is now the largest foreign investor in the United States, surpassing Britain and other European countries. Japan has also become the world's largest donor to developing countries and is taking an increasing interest in global development. As the world becomes more multipolar, Japan will continue as an influential economic force.

2
Before You Leave

VISAS

Short-term Visas

Visa regulations for Japan have changed in recent years. Westerners may now enter Japan without a visa for up to ninety days on what is called a **tourist permit**.

● After ninety days you must leave the country — there is no extension for a tourist permit.

If you take the time to obtain a **tourist visa** from a Japanese consulate outside of Japan, you are eligible for a ninety-day extension after your initial visa has expired. You also have the option of changing your status by applying for a **cultural** or **working visa**.

Some people come to Japan to study a particular aspect of Japanese culture, such as martial arts, the tea ceremony, or the Japanese language. It is possible to get a cultural visa to pursue these studies through the arts school you plan to attend. Working visas are obtained by foreigners who are hired by Japanese companies. Both the Japanese companies and art schools provide all the necessary paperwork for the appropriate visa.

People travelling to Japan on business for a period not exceeding 180 days may apply for a **short-term commercial visa**. Requirements for both the tourist and the commercial visa include:

a valid passport
a completed visa application in duplicate
two passport photos
a guarantee of financial responsibility, including return fare (or simply transportation out of the country).

In addition, the commercial visa also requires a letter (in duplicate) signed by an officer of your firm specifying in detail what you expect to do in Japan and the name and address of a Japanese business reference in Japan. You will also need a sponsor, a Japanese citizen or company to guarantee your flight out of Japan if you are found to be an undesirable.

In certain cases applications must be sent to Japan for approval. Additional papers such as an annual report of the company or a letter of guarantee from a Japanese firm which has close business relations with the applicant's company may be requested.

Long-term visas

A person travelling to Japan to take up a supervisory or executive post in a branch, representative office, or joint venture must have a **long-term commercial visa**. All the requirements listed for the short-term visa apply and should cover the applicant's accompanying family.

For the long-term visa, the consulate requires a statement in duplicate from the applicant's firm describing the nature of the company in Japan, the responsibilities and salary of the applicant, and a list of all the non-Japanese employees, their length of stay, and their positions within the company. (Ask the Japanese consul for forms prior to departure.)

ENTRY REGULATIONS AND RESTRICTIONS

Health regulations

A smallpox vaccination certificate is no longer necessary. If you are travelling from an infected area to Japan, cholera and/or yellow fever shots will be required. Protection against typhus, typhoid, and polio is desirable, even though these diseases are not common in Japan. It is also advisable to keep up your tetanus boosters and give your children the normal childhood inoculations.

Currency restrictions

There are no currency restrictions for a visitor coming to or leaving the country, but the Ministry of Finance reserves the right to impose a limit depending on the international economic situation.

Customs regulations

Customs clearance is slow but courteous. You may bring in four hundred cigarettes or one hundred cigars or half a pound of tobacco. You may also bring in three bottles of liquor, two ounces of perfume, and two timepieces (clocks or watches). Firearms, narcotics, and vegetable matter are not allowed, but personal medications are, of course, though it is advisable to have prescriptions or a doctor's statement with you for any which contain narcotics.

Regulations on accompanying household goods are very lenient. Anything that will follow you within six months of your arrival must be declared on a special form — unaccompanied luggage and everything shipped separately (car, pets, etc). New and unused appliances are subject to duty but not used ones. The automotive division of the **Japan External Trade Organization (JETRO),** can give you full details on importing cars to Japan.

PETS

If you plan to bring a pet with you to Japan, you will need proof of a **rabies inoculation** not less than 30 days or more than 150 days prior to your arrival in Japan. You will also need your vet's certificate of good health, which must be certified by the proper official in the Japanese consulate. Dogs are subject to quarantine for between 14 and 180 days at the discretion of the Japanese veterinary quarantine officer. There is no quarantine for cats. Get information on regulations covering animal entry from a Japanese consulate or the Royal Society for the Prevention of Cruelty to Animals (RSPCA) in your area.

Quarantine authorities are polite; English-speaking veterinarians and kennels are available. The biggest drawback in taking a pet is the housing difficulty they present. Many apartments and houses do not allow tenants to have pets. With housing in short supply this should be a serious consideration.

CLOTHING

Adults
Clothing for each season in Japan is much like what you would wear in Europe or North America at the same latitude. The Japanese tend to be very fashion conscious and spend a great amount of money on designer and brand name clothes, footwear, and accessories. Generally a great deal of attention is paid to how one looks.

Men may dress informally outside the office, but shirts, ties, and jackets are customary for business and lunch appointments. Fine quality dark blue or grey suits are the national uniform for the Japanese middle class business; brown suits are rarely seen. The millions of office workers who once wore nothing but white shirts are now seen more and more in stripes and pastels, but the higher up the ladder you go, the more formal the attire.

Black suits are worn for funerals and weddings, with a black tie for the former and a white tie for the latter.

For women, conservative blouses and skirts are the norm in the business world. Mature Japanese women usually wear skirts, often full, which make kneeling on the **tatami** floors of homes and restaurants easier. Dresses are not as popular as in Western countries. Young women are often seen in slacks nowadays, and teenagers wear blue jeans as they do all over the world.

Kimonoes are worn only on special occasions such as weddings and holiday celebrations. The **yukata**, the kimono's comfortable cotton cousin, is worn casually inside the home and at resorts. Hotels generally provide their clients with yukata bearing the establishment's symbol, much like a logo. While on vacation patrons will wear their hotel's yukata as they relax at the resort and even if they go out on the town. This custom serves to provide individuals with a means of identifying other members of their 'hotel family' and thus with the comfortable environment of a family group away from home.

The Japanese are becoming taller and bigger because of nutritional improvements since the end of the Second World War. Clothes are available in most sizes, but Japanese body structure is still basically small. The sleeves of Japanese shirts and the length of slacks and skirts are often too short for Westerners, but good tailor-made shirts, suits, blouses, and skirts are available for a price. Many businesspeople make a quick trip to Hong Kong to stock up on the inexpensive tailor-made clothes available there. Tall and large-sized Westerners may have a problem finding clothes that suit them (see the chart on clothing sizes, page 23).

The Japanese are bothered more by hot weather than cold, and although apartments frequently have air-conditioning, they probably will not have central heating. Floors are often cold in winter, so slippers, warm socks, and stockings are a necessity. Dressing in layers of clothing is the best approach. Undershirts or vests for men and women are widely worn by the Japanese and are a good idea. Women will find jackets useful, as well as warm coats to keep out the wind. Ski clothes are needed for winter sports.

Footwear is likely to be your biggest clothing problem. Slip-ons or shoes that do not require lacing are highly recommended. You will take your shoes off and put them back on many times each day in homes, restaurants, temples, and other places and may find tying and untying laces annoying and time-consuming. It is also important to have shoes that are comfortable for walking. Most people walk miles each day as they move between public transport stops and their home, office, or shops.

Clothing size differences

Shirts and Collars

Japanese	36	37	38	39	40	41	42
American and English	14	$14^1/_2$	15	$15^1/_2$	16	$16^1/_2$	17

Men's Suits, Overcoats and Sweaters

Japanese	S		M		L		LL
American and English	34	36	38	40	42	44	46

Women's Dresses and Suits

Japanese	9	11	13	15	17	19	21
American	10	12	14	16	18	20	22
English	32	34	36	38	40	42	44

Men's Shoes

Japanese	$24^1/_2$		26		$27^1/_2$	28	29
American	$5^1/_2$	$6^1/_2$	$7^1/_2$	$8^1/_2$	$9^1/_2$	$10^1/_2$	$11^1/_2$
English	5	6	7	8	9	10	11

Women's Shoes

Japanese	23	$23^1/_2$	24	$24^1/_2$	25	$25^1/_2$	26
American	6	$6^1/_2$	7	$7^1/_2$	8	$8^1/_2$	9
English	$4^1/_2$	5	$5^1/_2$	6	$6^1/_2$	7	$7^1/_2$

Keep in mind that you will need sturdy shoes since road and path surfaces are often rough.

Large and wide shoe sizes are generally unavailable in Japan. Men's shoes come only in two widths and only up to size 11; women's go only up to size 9. Western-style shoes are available, but since they are manufactured in Japan and cut for the Japanese, they tend to be small. If you are hard to fit, take a good supply of footwear.

Children's clothes

Styles and colours of clothing for small children are delightful. Cut larger than most Western styles, they are roomy and allow for plenty of movement.

Design and quality may be poor in inexpensive stores; in large department stores the quality is good but prices are higher than in most other countries. We suggest taking rugged play clothes, wash-and-wear pants, and sturdy shoes for children, though you may also want to try out the cleverly designed Japanese canvas shoes and other special items. There are many very useful accessories such as the **ombu**, a harness for carrying young children, and excellent fold-up prams and car seats.

3
Arriving in Japan

TRANSPORT

From the airport

Flight time to Tokyo varies according to route and weather but is roughly eighteen hours from Europe and eleven hours from the west coast of the USA. Tokyo time is Greenwich Mean Time plus nine hours, or Eastern Standard Time plus fourteen hours.

On the plane you will be required to fill out a disembarkation-embarkation card. The disembarkation half is presented to the immigration officer when you arrive in Japan. The embarkation half is stapled into your passport and has to be submitted to the immigration officer when you depart.

There are three international airports in Japan — Narita and Haneda in Tokyo and Itami in Osaka — but almost all international flights coming to Japan land at Narita Airport. Smaller airports serve all the major cities.

Narita Airport

Narita Airport is forty miles from central Tokyo and maintains rigid security. Security forces are very visible, and no one gets in to the airport without having his or her passport checked; bags are often searched. Large-scale and occasionally violent demonstrations by displaced farmers and radical political parties took place at Narita when it was first built, and conflict still occurs now and then as the facility is expanded.

Transport to Tokyo includes train, taxi, and airport limousine. The cheapest and easiest is the relatively new Narita Express, which runs to downtown Tokyo. Taxis are also available, but the fare can be well over £100. The airport limousine bus costs about £12, but is slower than the Narita Express. Leaving every fifteen minutes or so, it takes anywhere from an hour and a half to three hours, depending on the traffic. It stops at major hotels and train stations in downtown Tokyo.

Haneda Airport
This serves all domestic flights and some international routes, mainly those from Asia. It takes between fifteen to forty-five minutes to make the eleven-mile trip from Haneda to Tokyo by taxi, bus, or monorail.

Itami Airport (Osaka International)
This serves the Kansai area. It is about thirty minutes from Osaka, forty minutes from Kobe, and an hour from Kyoto. Buses leave about every fifteen minutes (see the description of the Kansai area in chapter 12 for bus arrival and departure points).

Public transport
Public transport in Japan is modern and extremely efficient but tends to be very crowded in metropolitan areas. The main problem for foreigners is the language barrier which makes the use of public transport difficult and confusing. The amount of English used to designate carriers, stops and routes varies with the type of transport. For instance, metropolitan train and subway stations usually have signs in English, but bus stops will not necessarily be similarly marked. This means that bus services can be more difficult for those who do not read and speak Japanese. Non-Japanese speakers, however, should not be deterred since one can still take advantage of the convenience of public transport, even if one is not very familiar with the language.

Subways and commuter trains
Japan has an excellent rail network of over 16,000 miles. Commuter trains and subways tend to be the preferred means of travel for business people and are punctual to the minute. They are invariably clean and well maintained. Millions of people take advantage of Japan's public transport system every day. Tokyo's Shinjuku station alone sees two million people pass through its halls daily. During rush hours, 0730-0930 and 1700-1900, coaches are literally packed with commuters. At a few of the busiest stations there are actually 'pushers' to help cram people into the trains.

Many stations contain huge multilevel shopping centres; you can walk through the underground mall surrounding the station for hours. If you get lost, simply ask someone for the trains (**densha**).

To use the subway, you purchase a ticket as you enter; the cost varies according to your destination. In Tokyo, bilingual subway maps are available at tourist information offices. They can prove indispensable in deciphering the fare maps above the ticket-dispensing machines. If you do not have a bilingual map, be sure to have your destination written down in Japanese. By simply matching the characters of your destination to those on the fare schedule you can see how much to pay for your ticket. Another option is to buy the cheapest fare and pay the rest at the fare adjustment window at the exit gate of your destination. When you enter the boarding area, your ticket will be punched. Keep the ticket; you must surrender it as you leave the station at your destination.

At most stations in metropolitan areas the stops are printed in English as well as Japanese. If you pass your stop, just get out at the next one and go back.

There are occasionally Japanese men on very crowded trains who enjoy rubbing up against women for the sexual thrill. Passive Japanese women rarely do anything in retaliation. The best strategy for victimised women is to embarrass and berate the offender in an angry voice and attempt to move away. It does not matter what language is used; the message is universal. On late trains you may encounter individuals who have had far too much to drink during a long evening with fellow workers. Rarely are they a serious problem although they can be annoying.

Cross-country trains

To travel in Japan one usually takes a train which can vary from a local that stops at every station to the famous high-speed **Shinkansen**.

There are three types of tickets:

● **Unreserved** are regular class, first come, first served seating. Depending on where and when you go, your train could be empty, but don't count on it. Popular runs are usually filled and have standing room only.

● **Reserved seats** cost a little bit more but are worth it, especially if you are travelling with children. The

● **Green car** is first class service and will cost a great deal more

If possible, buy tickets in advance from a private travel service; this is so much easier than trying to do it in the confusion of the station. Also, a travel service is more likely to have someone who speaks English. On the day of travel, make sure you have all the details written down in Japanese and allow yourself plenty of time to find the right platform and train. The conductors on the platform will be helpful in finding the appropriate section of the platform to wait for your particular railway carriage.

With unreserved seating you buy a ticket for distance only, not for a specific train. You can get on and off at any stop along the way as long as you reach your destination before the ticket expires — check the date printed on it.

The Shinkansen is much more expensive than its slower cousin but shaves hours off transportation times. Travelling at a maximum speed of 130 miles per hour, the trip between Tokyo and Fukuoka in Kyushu, a distance of 731 miles, is completed in less than seven hours.

During national holidays an incredibly large number of Japanese travel. Every train is packed to overflowing. Avoid train travel at these times or be sure to book well in advance.

If you plan to taken an extended vacation by rail while in Japan, a **JapanRail Pass** could be a good idea. This alternative is discussed in the Travel section of Chapter 11.

Buses

Buses are an inexpensive means of transport but are difficult to use if you don't read Japanese. Route maps use Japanese symbols with Arabic numerals. At stops the numbers of the buses which take on passengers will be listed on the sign along with a timetable. Do get your destination written down so that it can be shown to the bus driver and other passengers who can help identify your stop.

There are two types of buses in Japan. On one you pay a set fare of about Y160. These are most common in and around Tokyo and Osaka. The other type has fares based on the distance travelled. For this kind of bus, the usual procedure is to board at the rear door and take a ticket from a little machine. When you want to get off, check the fare chart by the front door exit and pay the amount which corresponds to your ticket number.

Taxis

Taking taxis will lessen the strain on your nerves and blood pressure when shopping or sightseeing. You can arrange for their services by the hour through hotel doormen, or flag them down in the street, although they do not always stop. Taxi ranks can also be found at hotels and all train stations.

If a taxi is unoccupied, a red sign will be lit in the window in front of the passenger seat. It is often difficult to find taxies in the rain or on paydays and sometimes foreigners will have more difficulty than Japanese. Because of the language difficulties non-Japanese passengers often present, drivers prefer Japanese to foreign clients. Thus, don't be surprised if a number of cabs pass you by before one stops.

An important point to understand is that cabs are entered from the kerb side and doors are controlled remotely by the driver, do don't try to open or close them yourself. Rates are about Y3000 an hour or the meter charge, whichever is higher. Taxi drivers are not tipped unless they carry luggage or provide other special services. Many cabbies work sixteen-hour double shifts, and have to carry a certain number of passengers each day, so they drive like crazy to make their quotas.

If possible, look for a driver-owned cab (called **kojin**). The **kanji** symbol indicates these special cabs. Kojin drivers have to be **yu** drivers, that is, tested as excellent, in order to get owner-driver permits; they also have to have had long experience in driving the streets of Tokyo. The kojin are less garish in colour than fleet taxis, and can also be distinguished by a sign on the roof showing the two kojin characters. The characters also appear on the door in parentheses.

If you are travelling alone or without someone who knows Japanese, it is a good idea to have your destination written out for you in Japanese, including the telephone number, and to carry your hotel or home address. Since most drivers do not speak any English, this can make for a much easier trip and return journey. Cars can also be hired with English-speaking drivers but the cost is much higher. Addresses are very confusing in Japan, and even experienced cabbies sometimes get lost. If your driver does, ask him to telephone (**denwa shite**, pronounced den-wah she-tay) your destination for directions.

Car rentals

There are over 150 car rental agencies in Japan, with a wide variety of vehicles available. Prices are slightly higher than in other countries. Many of the offices are closed on Sundays and national holidays. A number of agencies, including Hertz, Honda, and Nippon Rent-a-Car, have branches in all major cities, at airports, and at major hotels. An international or Japanese licence is required, and the driver must be aged at least eighteen.

MONEY MATTERS

Currency

The Japanese unit of currency is the **yen**. Notes come in different sizes and colours and in steps of 1,000, 5,000 and 10,000 yen. Coins are made of aluminium, copper or silver, and are available as 1, 5, 10, 50, 100, 500 yen pieces. Since 30th August 1971, the yen has been allowed to float freely. The exchange rate changes constantly and is printed daily in all English- language newspapers and posted at all major hotels and banks. In mid-1992 the rate was about Y237 to one pound sterling.

Banking

Anyone living in Japan for an extended period will want to open a deposit account at a Japanese bank. Such bank accounts can be opened with as little as Y100. Current accounts and personal cheques are not common. Cash is the preferred medium of exchange because it is quickest and easiest. Due to the low incidence of crime, carrying large amounts of cash around is considered preferable to having to wait at the grocery checkout. Bank machines are just beginning to make their entrance in the Japanese banking system and are not as popular as in Britain since they have been installed inside banks and are only available during normal banking hours. Bills can be paid automatically through your bank. Post offices also offer banking services. You may want to go with a Japanese friend when first opening an account; main branches of large banks will probably have banking information in English, but not always.

Credit cards and traveller's cheques

All the major credit cards and traveller's cheques may be used in the larger Japanese establishments. Most of the Western-style hotels and their shops will exchange traveller's cheques, US dollars, and pounds sterling. Cashier's cheques are not advised; using them is time-consuming (clearance can take as much as a month) and involves a great deal of red tape.

Tipping

Tipping is not customary in Japan. In hotels a 10-20 percent surcharge is added for service. In restaurants, if the bill exceeds Y2500 per person, 10 percent is added. Never try to tip someone who has helped show you the way somewhere or has done you a kindness. He or she will feel insulted; just offer a warm thanks.

Duty-free shopping

You can buy as much as you want from designated tax-free stores in large cities, but be sure to obtain Tax-Free Certificates on any major purchase to show to customs when you leave Japan. Take your passport with you when you make such purchases.

Taxes

With each revision, the Japanese tax system has become increasingly complex. There are both direct and indirect taxes imposed on individuals and corporations by both national and local governments.

Of special interest to foreigners are, of course, the income tax and the various consumer taxes. The latter include taxes on travel, postage stamps, food, lodging, entertainment, cars, tobacco, petrol and utilities. There are also luxury taxes on various commodities.

In April 1989 Japan instituted a new 3 percent consumption tax (rather like VAT) on everything from stamps to college tuition. This tax has caused many problems and much confusion because of the ambiguities and complexities of the law.

● Generally, the income tax authorities consider an individual living and working in Japan for a year or more as a resident.

Japanese authorities will tax all income received by residents, from both national and international sources. Nonresidents are people who reside in Japan for less than a year; they pay tax only on income from sources within Japan.

Whatever taxes corresponding to Japanese income tax you pay outside Japan can be claimed as a credit against the Japanese income tax, with certain limitations. A new arrival should check with local sources about prefecture and area-specific regulations.

You should also obtain information regarding your tax status in your home country while you reside in Japan. Your embassy or consulate has the necessary forms and will also answer any tax questions you may have.

IMMIGRATION REGULATIONS

Extending your visa

If you plan to stay longer in Japan than your present visa allows, go to the Immigration Office within thirty days of the expiration date (not before that) to request an extension. You will need a letter from your sponsor (except in the case of a tourist visa) guaranteeing further support and repatriation and giving the reason for the extension.

It can take up to two months for you to receive your new visa, but the immigration official will stamp your passport stating you have applied for it.

Alien registration

Within sixty days of arrival you, and all members of your family over the age of fourteen, must register at the ward office (city administrative) of your city. (In Tokyo and other major urban areas, this would be one of the smaller cities, or **shi**, within the metropolis, for example, Mitaka-shi in Tokyo, Matsubara City in Osaka.) Bring your passports and three passport photos for each family member. You will complete a form in duplicate, be fingerprinted, and receive your **Alien Registration Card**. The card is good for five years, after which time it can be renewed.

Surprisingly, there is no fee for an Alien Registration card, but be sure to register before the sixty-day period expires; otherwise, you are in for all sorts of problems. At the very least you will have to write a **gomen nasai** (I'm sorry) letter, stating that you are totally at fault and humbly begging for forgiveness.

All foreigners in Japan must carry their passports or Alien Registration Cards at all times. If you have an accident or any other official encounter and you do not have your passport or card with you, you will find yourself, according to the Japanese, in serious trouble — which means you will be spending a very lengthy time trying to explain yourself and apologising.

Every change of address or status while you are in Japan must be reported to the ward office within fourteen days so that it can be entered on your card. Your must, of course, immediately report a lost or stolen card.

If you should have a baby while in Japan, find out in advance from your consulate or embassy the rules for registering the child. The Japanese are very fussy about procedures; red tape is often prodigious.

Reentry permits

If you plan to leave Japan but return, you must get a reentry permit. The **single reentry permit** allows you to reenter Japan once. The **multiple reentry permit** allows for unlimited returns while it is valid (until your present visa expires). Multiple reentry permits are, however, more expensive and have an expiration date. For travellers only returning a single time, a single reentry permit is more economical.

Reentry permits can be obtained at any immigration office in Japan, for a fee. Please note, however, that if you have a single-entry visa and leave the country without a reentry permit, your Alien Registration Card will become invalid.

Immigration offices

Immigration offices are overworked and understaffed. At the Tokyo office nearly a thousand people are processed every day. The lines are long and the office is small. Be prepared to spend a good part of the day waiting; have all your documents in order, and be polite. It is a privilege to stay in Japan and the officials can deny that privilege to anyone they do not like (see the Useful Addresses appendix for addresses of immigration offices in the various cities).

STREET ADDRESSES

In Japan there are no street addresses as Westerners know them, but the Japanese have their own system, which has these divisions: **ku, machi, cho, chome**, and **banchi**.

> **Ku** is the ward;
> **machi** is the town within the **ku**;
> **cho** is the village within the **machi**;
> **chome** is the block (or it may be several blocks) within the **cho**;
> **banchi** is the building number within the **chome**. Traditionally, buildings are assigned numbers as they are built rather than according to location so sometimes the system can be quite confusing.

In Tokyo, as in most large cities, there are also districts like the Ginza, Marunouchi and Shinjuku.

KEEPING IN TOUCH

Telephones

Overseas calls
Placing overseas calls from Japan is relatively easy. International calls can be made from the green, card/coin public telephones with an 'International Domestic Card/Coin Telephone' legend on the front panel of the coin box. These telephones are located in airport lobbies, major hotels, and most large train stations. They can be used for ISD (see below), reverse charge, and credit card calls. Telephone cards are inserted in a special slot in these telephones and are debited for the amount of the call. Cards are available at all telephone stores and at the numerous card-vending machines. They range from 500 yen to 10,000 yen, 1,000 yen being the most common.

1. ISD (**International Subscriber Dialling**) calls. After picking up the receiver, insert several Y100 coins or a Japanese telephone card. Dial 001 + country code + area code + local telephone number. Country codes can be found in the telephone book.

2. **Reverse charge and credit card calls**. Insert a Y10- or 100- coin or a Japanese telephone card before dialling. Next dial 0051 and book

your call with the KDD operator. KDD (Kokusai Denshin Denwa) deals with all international calls. There are English-speaking operators to assist you when needed. Upon completing the call and replacing the receiver, your coin or card will be returned.

In most airports and large hotels, there is also the new **Home Country Direct** service. Just push the button of the country you wish to call.

Economy and discount rates for direct dialled calls are available from 1900 in the evening to 0800 in the morning daily and all day on Sundays and national holidays. These rates are not available for operator-assisted calls.

Local calls

If you are in the same city as the number you are dialling, simply dial the individual telephone number. If you are calling to another city, you must dial that city's area code before the telephone number.

Public telephones come in a variety of colours; the green ones take Japanese telephone cards as well as coins. Local calls cost Y10 for three minutes of service. The further away you call outside the local area, the more your call will cost. To use a pay phone, lift the receiver, insert a Y10- or Y100-coin, and dial your number. More than one coin, or even a combination of coins and telephone card can be used in pay phones. The phone will use up the telephone cards first, then the Y100-coins, and finally the Y10-coins. Public telephones do not give change when Y100-coins are used. Before your time is up, a buzzer sounds to indicate more coins must be inserted.

Telegrams

Overseas telegrams are handled by KDD — Tokyo office, Tel: (03) 270-5111 — or at post offices or major hotels. There is a seven-word minimum. Urgent telegrams cost double and lettergrams are half the ordinary rate.

Postal services

The International Post Office and Customs Office is open from eight in the morning until eight in the evening, and English-speaking clerks are available to help you. Tel: (03) 241-4891. Stamps may be bought at hotels, post offices, and at any small shop that displays a red-and-white double-capped 'T' sing. Red postboxes are for ordinary mail, blue ones for express mail or special delivery. In Tokyo if there are two slots in

Some key telephone services

Some important numbers (answered in Japanese) to note are the following:

Police	Tel: 110
Fire/Ambulance	Tel: 119
Time of Day	Tel: 117
Directory Assistance	Tel: (area code) + 104
Area Code Information	Tel: 105

Telephone Information
In addition to 'Information in English' (described on page 40), **Japan Travel Phone** offers English-language travel information and assistance in solving problems from nine in the morning to five in the evening daily.

For eastern Japan	Tel: (0120)	222-800
For western Japan	Tel: (0120)	444-800
For Tokyo	Tel: (03)	502-1461
For Kyoto	Tel: (075)	371-5649

the red box, the right-hand one is for Tokyo, the left is for everywhere else.

Airmail to Europe or the USA may take only six days; however, it can sometimes be delayed so long in the Tokyo bottleneck that delivery may take as long as nine days. For sea mail allow six to eight weeks. Parcel post may take up to eight weeks. Most department stores will ship your purchases overseas. Mail service overseas from Japan is very efficient and quite safe (smaller packages mailed surface sometimes go by air).

Newspapers, periodicals, and books

Japan has four English-language newspapers: the *Japan Times*, the *Daily Yomiuri*, the *Asahi Evening News,* and the *Mainichi Daily News.* All of these are sold in major hotels and train stations. The *Japan Times* has the largest circulation and can be delivered to your home. The *International Herald Tribune* is now printed in Tokyo and is available daily. To subscribe, call (03) 201-0205. Other overseas newspapers are usually a day later and at least four times the newsstand price.

Two reliable and useful journals for business executives come out weekly: *The Japan Economic Journal* and the *Oriental Economist.* Two very good monthlies are *Business Tokyo* and *Venture Japan.* There is also now an *Asian Wall Street Journal*, and the American Chamber of Commerce of Japan puts out a monthly journal that is useful in monitoring the Japan business scene.

Time, Newsweek, and many other magazines are available at major hotels and in English-language bookstores, such as Kinokuniya in Shinjuku. *Newsweek* subscriptions can also be taken in Tokyo by calling (03) 478-6721.

English-language books can be found on sale in most large hotels. There are also a few large bookshops, like **Kinokuniya**, and a number of secondhand bookstores that carry English books.

Radio and television

The main radio station broadcasting in English is FEN (**Far East Network**), at 810kHz on the AM dial. This is maintained and operated by US forces stationed in Japan. FEN's hourly news reports, sports, and US radio programmes are an important link for the expatriate to the world outside Japan. Many Japanese radio stations broadcast English language programmes and may even have foreign DJs.

Many Japanese television sets come equipped with a bilingual switch, which enables you to watch and listen to certain shows in either language. Popular English and other foreign language films are shown once or twice a week. VCRs are popular and there are many video stores which offer both Japanese and English films. Some American television series are also broadcast but mostly between one and four in the morning. There are nightly news broadcasts which are simultaneously translated into English and can be heard via the bilingual switch. Special international events are being shown more often. Cable is available in the large cities — CNN is everywhere.

SECURITY

Insurance

According to Japanese law, foreign insurance companies that do not have branch offices in Japan cannot issue policies on persons and property in Japan. You can, of course, insure with British or other Western companies that do have licensed branches there.

The British and American Chambers of Commerce of Japan are useful sources of information on insurance and other personal and business matters. Personal insurance is recommended on household contents and liability for fire, earthquake, and windstorm damage. Fire is feared in this crowded land of paper and wood houses, especially since neither fire protection nor water supplies are adequate to the need. Earthquakes are frequent and though most are mild, strong quakes do occur. Therefore, the Japanese place great stress on earthquake preparedness. Windstorms and typhoons are also known to cause considerable damage.

Some people take out a **Broad Form Resident Theft** policy, a relatively inexpensive and valuable protection. Incidentally, if you injure an intruder in your home, you are subject to charges of assault and battery. You are expected to leave him to the police.

Health insurance
Regarding health insurance, anyone with a working visa may apply for coverage under Japanese National Health Insurance at the ward office in your residential area (see chapter 8 on health for more information).

You are responsible for the medical care of any staff you employ in your home. You will probably want to insure your household help for accidents and sickness. If you have school-age children, find out whether the school provides accident insurance. Not all schools do.

Police
Japan has an enviable police force; over 47 percent overall are university/college graduates — 50 percent in Tokyo, nearly 60 percent in Osaka, and an amazing 76.4 percent in Hiroshima. Japan has long been noted for the quiet efficiency of its police and its extraordinarily low crime rate. Japanese police work closely with local communities, even in Tokyo; the neighbourhood **koban** (policebox) system gives the police unusually close and friendly rapport with each community.

Police boxes are small buildings located at strategic corners in each neighbourhood. The officers are assigned to a koban twenty-four hours a day. They take turns patrolling the district on bicycles. Almost none of Japan's few murders and robberies are committed with handguns, the ownership of which is strictly forbidden. While the policemen themselves are generally armed, they almost never use their weapons in the line of duty.

Japan's elite riot police are noted for their discipline, toughness, and restraint. Their training includes the delicate arts of the tea ceremony and flower arranging, as well as advanced training in judo, kendo and karate.

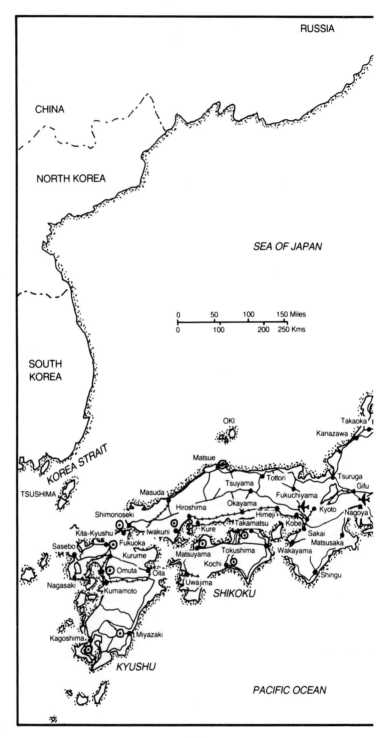

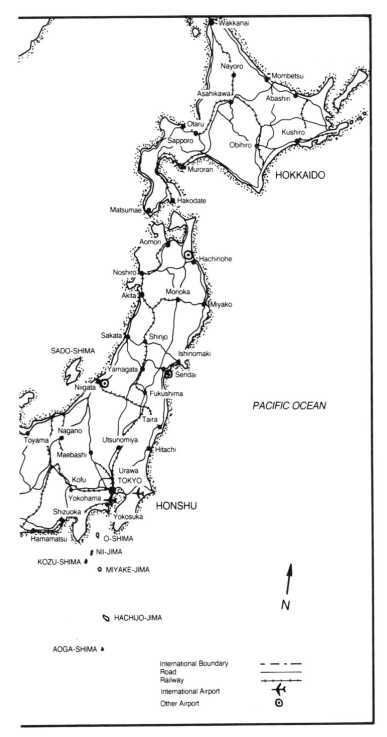

RESOURCES FOR VISITORS

Help on arrival
Information in English is a telephone service provided in Tokyo and Yokohama by NTT (Nippon Telephone and Telegraph, which deals with all calls inside Japan). This service can help you with useful numbers and information on any aspect of living or travelling in Japan. They will provide addresses of hospitals and other agencies that help with various kinds of problems. Phones lines are open Monday to Saturday from 1000 to 1900.

At Narita Airport(0476)28-1010
In Tokyo(03)201-1010
In Yokohama(045)322-1010

Tourist information centres
The **Japanese National Tourist Organization** (JNTO) is friendly, and its helpful English-speaking staff will provide information, maps, schedules, and directions for travel around Japan. These offices, which are open from Monday to noon on Saturday, are located at the following addresses:

Narita Airport
Airport Terminal building, Narita, Chiba pref. Tel: (0476) 32-8711.

Tokyo
Kotani Building, 6-6 Yurakucho 1-chome, Chiyoda-ku, Tokyo. Tel: (03) 502-1461.

Kyoto
Kyoto Tower building, First floor, Higashi-Shiokojicho, Shimogyo-ku, Kyoto. Tel: (075) 371-5649.

4
Coping with the Language

MEANINGS AND NUANCES

In Japan, language is inextricably interwined with social life. Language is not so much an expression of ideas as an expression of sociality. For a Japanese to speak incorrectly, for instance too informally or too familiarly with a senior, is considered antisocial behaviour. Although speech is often considered a secondary means of communication, incorrect use of the spoken word can mean great loss of respect for the speaker.

The Japanese derive meaning from the context of a conversation — *who* is speaking, *how* the message is delivered, and the situations in which the parties are involved — rather than the actual words. For the Japanese, what is said is not nearly as important as *how* it is said. For a more thorough discussion of this topic, see chapter 5.

The importance placed on the manner of speaking is reflected in the language. Although Japanese grammar is fairly straightforward and there are few exceptions to the rules, the words themselves are altered according to the amount of respect or familiarity one wishes to express. Such changes have no real equivalents in English and so can be difficult to adjust to for language students. For example, the verb **iku** (to go) is informal and might be used in a sentence like 'The child goes.' When the formal suffix is added, the verb becomes **ikimasu**, which reflects more respect and would be appropriate for a sentence like, 'The woman goes.' When a student says 'The teacher goes,' for instance, the verb changes yet again to indicate even more respect, **i'te gozaimasu**. The closest English translation would be, 'He respectably goes.'

To speak Japanese well one must be perfectly in tune with the intricacies and subtleties of Japanese society. Thus, though it is easy for the student of Japanese to get his or her idea across, it is exceedingly difficult to do it with the correct amount of deference and socially important expressions of respect.

HIRAGANA, KATAKANA AND RŌMAJI

I Basic Syllables:

Vowel, Consonant plus vowel and **n**
Note: The syllables **yi, ye, wi, wu** and **we** do not occur in modern Japanese.

The *kana* to the left are *hiragana*; *katakana* are in parentheses.

v \ c	a あ (ア)	i い (イ)	u う (ウ)	e え (エ)	o お (オ)
k	ka か (カ)	ki き (キ)	ku く (ク)	ke け (ケ)	ko こ (コ)
s	sa さ (サ)	shi し (シ)	su す (ス)	se せ (セ)	so そ (ソ)
t	ta た (タ)	chi ち (チ)	tsu つ (ツ)	te て (テ)	to と (ト)
n	na な (ナ)	ni に (ニ)	nu ぬ (ヌ)	ne ね (ネ)	no の (ノ)
h	ha は (ハ)	hi ひ (ヒ)	fu ふ (フ)	he へ (ヘ)	ho ほ (ホ)
m	ma ま (マ)	mi み (ミ)	mu む (ム)	me め (メ)	mo も (モ)
y	ya や (ヤ)	■	yu ゆ (ユ)	■	yo よ (ヨ)
r	ra ら (ラ)	ri り (リ)	ru る (ル)	re れ (レ)	ro ろ (ロ)
w	wa わ (ワ)				o を (ヲ)
n, m	— ん (ン)				

II Modified Syllables:

Consonant plus basic vowel

g	ga が (ガ)	gi ぎ (ギ)	gu ぐ (グ)	ge げ (ゲ)	go ご (ゴ)
z	za ざ (ザ)	ji じ (ジ)	zu ず (ズ)	ze ぜ (ゼ)	zo ぞ (ゾ)
d	da だ (ダ)	ji ぢ (ヂ)	zu づ (ヅ)	de で (デ)	do ど (ド)
b	ba ば (バ)	bi び (ビ)	bu ぶ (ブ)	be べ (ベ)	bo ぼ (ボ)
p	pa ぱ (パ)	pi ぴ (ピ)	pu ぷ (プ)	pe ぺ (ペ)	po ぽ (ポ)

WRITING

Kanji and Hiragana

The Japanese did not use a writing system until the Chinese ideographic system was introduced by Buddhist monks in the sixth century BC. These ideographs have gradually developed from stylized pictures into quickly written characters and are called kanji. Kanji are the basis of modern written Japanese and can be as simple as a single horizontal stroke to signify the number one, to compound characters of thirty strokes.

The kanji of the Chinese system are richly connotative and well suited to the relatively simple language construction of Chinese, but they proved inadequate to express the very important nuances of spoken Japanese. Eventually, the Japanese simplified forty-six kanji into new symbols called kana, which stand for either vowels or simple consonant-vowel combinations. The kana thus express syllables and the resulting set of characters is called a syllabary. This syllabary, called hiragana, is used to supplement the kanji root characters and 'spell out' such elements as verb endings and the slight pronunciation differences which express different levels of respect and familiarity in the spoken language.

Katakana

In addition to kanji and hiragana, there is a second syllabary called *katakana*. Katakana are kana that differentiate words of Japanese origin from those of foreign origin. All words of Japanese origin are written using kanji or hiragana or a combination of the two. All foreign words employ katakana. Katakana can be interpreted as a kind of script or italicized hiragana. The symbols stand for exactly the same sounds as the kanji or hiragana, but they are even more simplified and can be recognized by their notably angular style.

Hiragana and katakana are employed when the Japanese wish to 'spell out' words syllabically and a working knowledge of them can prove useful. They are likely to be found on road signs, designating underground stations, in advertisements, and on menus and are common in everyday life. Flash cards are probably the best bet for learning the syllabaries and can be useful for whiling away long hours on an aeroplane.

The prospect of learning kanji can be somewhat daunting. More than 2,000 characters have been officially designated as commonly used and thousands more are studied by scholars. Certain kanji will prove very useful, and learning to recognize them should be top priority, if only to avoid some potentially embarrassing situations. These include **iriguchi** (entrance), **deguchi** (exit), **benjo** (toilet), **otoko** (man), **on'na** (woman), and the numbers.

If you plan to use public transport it would be very helpful to be able to recognise the kanji for regular destinations and to be able to write out your home or return address.

Although Japanese is a very complex language and not easily mastered, the effort you expend studying it will definitely be to your advantage. It is a matter of courtesy for a visitor to be able to speak at least some words and phrases in the language of the host country, and the Japanese are delighted and flattered when anyone tries. Furthermore, your mobility and access to the real Japan are greatly increased if you can talk with the people.

Number	Numeral	English
ichi	1	one
ni	2	two
san	3	three
shi	4	four
go	5	five
roku	6	six
shichi	7	seven
hachi	8	eight
kyuu	9	nine
ju	10	ten
ju-ichi	11	eleven
ju-ni	12	twelve
ju-san	13	thirteen
ni-ju	20	twenty
ni-ju-ichi	21	twenty-one
hyaku	100	hundred
sen	1,000	thousand
man	10,000	ten thousand

PRONUNCIATION

Japanese is not difficult to pronounce, unlike the neighbouring Chinese tonal language with its numerous dialects. The focus of Japanese is five vowel sounds. These are pronounced as follows:

A as in father	**san**
E as in ate	**sake**
I as in week	**kimono**

O as in most **obi**
U as in moon **mura**

There are also a few easily pronounced dipthongs such as *ai* as in kaiser (**samurai**) or *ei* as in rein (**geisha**). The first five kana of each of the syllabaries stand for these vowel sounds. All other sounds in the Japanese language are simply various consonants with these vowel sounds tacked on; for example, *ka, ki, ku, ke, ko, na, ni, nu, ne, no*, and so on. Learning the consonant sounds should generally be easy for English speakers since they are all commonly used in English.

Although it is fairly easy to sound out Japanese words once you have learned the kana, recognising supposedly familiar words that have been written in katakana can be surprisingly difficult. Being able to read the words is only half the battle; you must also be able to put the parts together and work out what they are referring to. For example, if you read the katakana characters for 'Re-Su-To-Ra-N,' you still need to put them together into the word *restaurant*. These hybrid words are called **gairaigo**; the word **gai** means foreign; **rai** means come; **go** means word (literally, 'words that come from outside'). Try these **gairaigo** for practice:

Ha-N-Ba-Ga	=	hamburger
Sa-N-Do-I-Chi	=	sandwich
U-I-Su-Kii	=	whisky
Bi-Ru Ga-De-N	=	beer garden
A-Pu-Ru Pa-I	=	apple pie
Pu-Ra-To-Ho-Mu	=	platform
Sho-Pi-N-Gu Se-N-Ta	=	shopping centre
Ma-Ku-Do-Na-Ru-Do	=	mcDonald's

As with most languages, a few pronunciation irregularities exist. These can be observed in the kana tables provided, such as the shifts from *s* to *sh* and *h* to *f*, but these are quickly learned and easily mastered.

One notable difference between Japanese and English is that Japanese does not differentiate between the sounds *l* and *r*. Often the Japanese *r* is pronounced somewhere between the English *l* and *r*. The result is that words such as *red* and *led* and *rice* and *lice* are not distinguished.

Another point to keep in mind is that Japanese does not include consonant combinations. Thus any foreign word which is written out in kana will be altered to fit the existing written language structure. The result is that such words as *bird* and *bad* are both written and pronounced in katakana as 'ba-do'.

Pronouncing words in Japanese is relatively easy when compared with English since every syllable receives equal stress. Most Japanese words have several syllables and nearly always end in a vowel, though sometimes the last letter is an *n*. To help get the feel of a word, pronounce it syllable by syllable: **ki-mo-no**, for example, or **Hi-ro-shi-ma**. If you run into a word with a consonant and a vowel separated by *y*, treat the combination as a single syllable: for example, **Kyushu** is pronounced cue-shoe.

LEARNING JAPANESE

There are many Japanese language schools located throughout the country, and traditional enrolment in a class is still the best way to make rapid progress in the early stages. A by-product of enrolling in a class is that you will meet and get to know others in your same situation.

Seek out a good tutor as well. If you want to learn quickly (before you lose heart!), you need classroom instruction *plus* home practice. In addition, listening to TV regularly will help your rhythm, cadence, and pronunciation, even if you do not understand the words. TV 'home dramas' — the equivalent of soaps — are relatively simple, entertaining, and easy to understand.

Purchase of or access to good reference books is also vital. Many books try to teach the beginner in romanised Japanese. Although this can be handy for people who only wish to speak the language and have very little time, it can severely handicap the serious student since it develops a reliance on the romanisation and impedes the process of learning to read and write. If you hope to be even slightly literate, you should learn the kana and their use right from the start.

When choosing texts or dictionaries to begin your study, try to find ones that are careful to explain grammatical points and that approach the subject with a bit of humour. Vocabulary lists should be checked to be sure they include everyday words that you expect to use often. A basic kanji book can get you started with writing and recognising the symbols.

Although you should learn hiragana and katakana, it will be a long time until you will be efficient with a Japanese dictionary that uses kana listings. For looking up words quickly, there is nothing like your native alphabet.

LANGUAGE SCHOOLS

Language schools continuously advertise in all English-language newspapers and other publications. Choosing the right school depends on what you are looking for and to a great extent on how lucky you are in finding it. There are many schools to choose from and you will want to explore several options before you choose one. Here are some points to keep in mind when looking for a language school:

A checklist

- Does the school emphasise speaking, reading, or writing or does it give all three equal emphasis?

- Are teachers able to explain complex grammatical points in English?

- How much opportunity is there for individually tailored courses?

- What are the teacher/student ratios?

- Will there be opportunity for extra help from the teachers or assistance in finding a tutor?

- What are the class materials like? Expensive text books or xeroxed sheets?

- Do facilities include audio-visual or individualized audio-cassette capabilities?

These are just a few points to consider when the time comes to make your decision. To help get you started, here is a brief list of some of the better known Japanese language institutes.

Leading language schools in Japan

Berlitz
Berlitz has over forty schools in cities throughout Japan, including Tokyo, Osaka, Nagoya, Kyoto, Fukuoka, Hiroshima, and Sapporo. Call their Tokyo office for more information: (03) 222-5351.

Bi-Lingual
Bi-Lingual has about twenty schools throughout Japan: in the Tokyo area, call (03) 780-5321; in the Nagoya area, call (052) 241-6231; and in the Osaka area, call (06) 362-9671.

ECC Foreign Language Institute
In the Tokyo Shibuya-ku area, call (03) 409-1300, or in Shinjuku-ku, (03) 268-4181. In the Nagoya area, call (052) 961-0144; in the Kyoto area, call (075) 252-1430; and in the Osaka area, call (06) 341-3287.

Linguarama Executive Language Schools
In the Tokyo area, call (03) 581-5634; in the Osaka area, the number is (06) 721-8978.

5
Coping with the Culture

INTRODUCTION

In discussing Japanese culture, indeed, in discussing any culture, the dangers of generalisation and stereotyping are ever present. There are exceptions to almost every rule and infinite variety within every culture. But certain general comments will help us to prepare for an encounter with values and forms of behaviour different from our own, and be ready to understand them rather than simply react to them. In speaking of 'the Japanese' we need always to remember that not all Japanese individuals will fit the general comments being made.

On the surface, Japan looks westernised. Glass and steel skyscrapers dominate the Tokyo skyline; neatly uniformed workers perform their tasks side by side with futuristic robots on car assembly lines; brisk young executives swarm through the streets and into banks and office buildings: huge industrial plants spew forth pollution; farms are highly mechanised; and the motorways are jammed with the latest models of motor car. But, beneath the surface beats the heart of an ancient society firmly founded on traditional principles and mores.

The combination of the old with the new, the ugly with the beautiful — this is Japan. Like a visual paradox, the eye is drawn first to the modern, then to the traditional, and back and forth until the differences become blurred. At times individuals may seem to merge with the groups to which they belong and a Western eye, unable to detect much difference and individuality may see just a whirl of conformity. When one sees more than the superficial eye of the newcomer, however, one finds a rich cultural setting peopled by individuals brought up to a complex and intricate code of ritual and responsibility. Japan begins to appear as it really is, a rich tapestry, the product of modern practices and ancient customs woven together. Exploring the intricacies of this tapestry is one of the joys of living in Japan.

RELIGIONS AND PHILOSOPHIES

Japanese pragmatism

The Japanese tend to be pragmatists, adopting those aspects of philosophical or religious systems that reinforce their basic attitudes towards social responsibility and personal duty while providing better ways of dealing with contemporary issues. They assimilate new ideas just as they assimilate new technologies: they find applications for whatever is useful and discard all excess, even where religion is concerned.

A well-known Japanese saying is that one is 'born Shinto and buried Buddhist.' Between these two occasions one may take part in ceremonies with all kinds of religious origins. Teachings that, over time, have been introduced to Japan have not been adopted as whole systems of belief. Instead elements of them have been selected for their utility. Religion is not so much a code of belief and behaviour as a source of rites and rituals to be used in day to day situations.

Three philosophies dominate, Shinto, Buddhism, and Confucianism. Over the centuries, they have fused into a set of precise social rules, mores, and traditions unique to the People of the Rising Sun. Awareness of these aspects of Japanese culture and the resulting codes of conduct can provide helpful insights into Japanese ways of thought.

Shinto

Japan's indigenous religion is called Shinto. The basic tenet of Shinto is that every object, animate or inanimate, is home to **kami**, or gods. The result is a naturalistic religion which stresses harmony with one's environment. Shinto is polytheistic, allowing for the existence of a multitude of deities and providing ample room for various belief systems and the assimilation of new ideas. Over the centuries Shinto has provided fertile ground for Japan's pragmatic tendencies.

Shinto shrines can be recognised by the **torii** gate — two upright pillars with a crosspiece on top. There are more than 100,000 such shrines throughout the country, of all sizes and degrees of opulence, from the huge **Meiji Shrine** in central Tokyo to thousands of small shrines along roads and paths. They have been erected wherever auspicious events have occurred or people have felt fit to honour the deities.

The Japanese visit shrines on auspicious occasions. During the New Year holiday most Shinto shrines are packed with people starting the year off right by invoking the gods. In every neighbourhood local shrines have their own festivals, attended by most of the people in the area.

Buddhism

During the sixth century AD, Buddhism was introduced to the Japanese Court by travelling monks from Korea. It was not until the tenth and eleventh centuries, however, that Buddhism began profoundly to influence Japanese ways of thought. At this time a series of Japanese and Chinese exchanges brought Buddhism to Japan in a form which became popular among the masses. From that time onward it has had a very strong influence on Japanese customs, culture, and philosophy.

Zen

Of the various sects of Buddhism, **Zen** has been particularly influential. Zen brings the mind, body, and spirit into a harmonious relationship through the stringent control of one's mental processes and emotional impulses. The great stress Zen places upon self-discipline made it very popular among the samurai class and it has had a profound effect on Japanese society by engendering the ideals of self-sacrifice and self-deprivation.

Confucianism

Introduced in the sixth century from China, Confucian ethics served to reinforce and codify the strong group ties of a rice-growing society. Confucianism stresses the importance of right thought and right behaviour and lays out a strict outline of social duty. Confucian teachings have served to reinforce the hierarchies and maintain the careful status distinctions that pervade Japanese society.

Christianity

Introduced in the sixteenth century, Christianity has attracted relatively few devout followers. The most visible aspect of Christianity is the current trend towards Western marriage ceremonies. They have become popular additions to nuptial proceedings but tend to be seen as supplementary to traditional Shinto rites rather than as replacements.

Bushido

Bushido, the Way of the Samurai, is the result of Japan's warrior class applying the teachings of Buddhism and Confucianism to their business — war. According to Zen Buddhist ideals, if one wishes to conquer others, one must first conquer one's self. This can only be done by strict self-discipline and through valiant inner struggle. The samurai also found the conformity to moral codes, refined manners, and absolute loyalty to one's lord propounded by Confucian teachings very attractive. Both were incorporated into a social, political and occupational code which still governs social behaviour.

For the Japanese, the prevalent attitude is likely to be one of a warrior engaging in spiritual battle. Inner strength is the way to victory over one's opponents, whether in the battlefield or at the negotiating table. The battle is not waged in the open, but rather behind the scenes and in the hearts of those involved. Negotiations follow strict forms of etiquette; lack of self-discipline is perceived as weakness and may be exploited as such. Personal honour is closely tied to adherence to strict rules of social conduct and interdependence.

HARMONIOUS RELATIONSHIPS

A definition of *Wa*

The Japanese word for 'harmony' is **wa**. The kanji for wa is derived from the characters for rice and mouth. When combined, these symbols connote mouths with rice or people with plenty of food. To the Japanese, having enough rice to eat means survival. Wa is the state of social balance and communal well-being that supports the close cooperation necessary to produce Japan's staple crop. Without wa, Japan would figuratively, if not literally, wither and die.

Wa is not always translated in a way which reflects its practical foundation. Thus Westerners are often surprised to find that an apparently harmonious relationship between Japanese turns out to be much less amiable than they thought. Beneath an extremely polite and self-sacrificing exterior run emotions and thoughts as real and personal as any experienced by a Westerner. For the Japanese the priority is to maintain external appearances, and suppress internal differences.

The conception of harmony which is embodied in wa does not necessarily signify a state of intrinsic balance, but rather a state of social compromise and practical cooperation, a condition for survival. You may hate your neighbour, but you must maintain good relations on the surface because when your rice is ready, you will need all the help you can get to harvest your fields. Appearance takes precedence over internal reality.

In business, wa is embodied in promotion practices and decision making processes. These minimize competitiveness and encourage smooth interaction at all levels of the company. Such manifestations do not signal a conflict-free company. In reality there may be intense competition between workgroups within the hierarchy. But it does mean that when a task is given priority by those in power, there will be strict rules for accomplishing it as efficiently as possible with a minimum of delay due to interpersonal politics.

Amae: the spirit of interdependence

Wa is the stuff of which the building blocks of Japanese society are built; **amae** is the mortar that holds them in place. Amae involves feelings of closeness and trusting dependency typified by the relationship between an infant and its mother.

Throughout their lives, the Japanese replicate relationships of reliance and interdependence. For individuals who join large companies, the company becomes the centre of their world, a new mother on whom they can depend, a benevolent being that will look after their interests and provide for their needs. For Westerners who see their employers only as sources of pay packets, this can be hard to understand.

Group identification

In Japan identity is defined not by one's individual achievements, but by the groups to which one belongs. The Japanese take into account the *who* and the *how* first, the *what* and the *why* later. Actions are mainly determined by situational factors. Individuals will alter their behaviour according to what the group (or Japanese society at large) expects from them. To adhere too strongly to a particular point of view may be seen as antisocial behaviour rather than as evidence of strong character.

Interdependence of group members is encouraged in young children and is a central feature of Japanese education. When children enter school they join a class where they will stay throughout their school years, and maintain strong ties long into adulthood.

Children soon learn that such relationships bring much responsibility, since any shame which befalls the individual reflects equally on his or her group. Individuals yield to the group and are taught by parents and teachers to value humility over personal expression. Later on, peer pressure replaces the influence of authority figures as the main force in keeping individuals from wandering too far from the group. Historically, the most serious sanction that one could suffer was the loss of membership in the group. In a nation of islands that for centuries had little contact with other countries and basically no immigration or emigration, such exclusion meant virtual exile in one's own home.

Uchi and soto

Uchi literally means house, and by extension one's family. It is used to refer to one's work family as well as blood relatives and can refer to anyone who is an insider or member of a group. **Soto**, in contrast, means outside and can refer to anyone who is an outsider or not a member of a particular group. In relationships between individuals who are uchi, it is vital to maintain wa. With those who are soto, one does not have to worry about the quality of interpersonal relations because for all practical purposes no relationship exists.

The boundaries between *uchi* and *soto* will vary depending on the situation. In one's private life, one's family is uchi while everyone else is soto. At work or on the playing field, one's colleagues and those not part of one's intimate circle are *soto*. On the international scene, all **Nihonjin** (Japanese) are uchi while all **Gaijin** (foreigners) are soto. Gaijin can never become fully integrated into Japanese society, and certainly can never become Japanese as for example someone can become an American.

Status and hierarchy

The stress placed on correct behaviour in Japanese society has led to strict guidelines for interaction with others. These guidelines can be followed only if individuals know their proper relationship with others. Whether one must defer to another, or is responsible to or for another will depend on the terms dictated by circumstance and the roles of those involved in a particular situation. Showing respect for age, rank, and status matters greatly to the Japanese.

Traditionally, Japanese society has been extremely hierarchical. An important aspect of Shinto is the highly ordered view of the world it provides. Everything, animate and inanimate, has its place. Confucian teachings spelled out relationships between men and women, lords and labourers, and elders and juniors. The strict Bushido code served to institutionalise the self-restraint necessary to maintain such formal structures.

In practical terms, this emphasis on status and hierarchy means that one should let the senior people in any situation speak first or take the lead. You will seriously risk damaging your standing and interfere with the development of personal and business relations if you fail to show respect for age and experience.

In Buddhist and Confucian traditions, men take precedence over women — men lead the way into rooms, theatres, lifts, cars and trains, and among men the senior person goes first. In introductions, precedence is based on age and rank. Don't expect a man to stand up for a woman, even if she if pregnant. In public conveyances, however, young girls will rise for older women, especially if they stand right in front of the younger ones.

Many Japanese are aware of the custom commonly known as 'ladies first' (lay-deesu fah-su-toe) and may attempt to follow it, especially if they have lived abroad, in an effort to make visiting women more comfortable. It might make them giggle, however, which would be a sign of their discomfort. One should pay no attention to the giggles and just accept this courteous gesture gracefully.

Responsibilities of the individual

At an early age Japanese children begin to learn what is considered proper and improper, and their responsibilities toward each other, their groups, and their society. Carrying out their obligations makes for complex and subtle social relations and calls for very strict self-control.

The Japanese believe that every individual is born into a set of circumstances that automatically bestow certain obligations, or **on** (pronounced own). One is automatically obligated to one's emperor, parents, and teachers, by virtue of their impact on the individual and his or her environment. These debts can never be fully repaid. Once **on** defines a relationship, that relationship remains constant throughout the life of those involved regardless of shifts in social status. A company president will always be in the debt of his grade school teachers, regardless of changes in social power or material wealth.

While one can never repay all **on**, there are some kinds of obligations which must be repaid and certain duties that individuals must fulfill in relation to those that they owe. These duties are called **giri** and serve to determine proper behaviour within Japan's social system. When one does not act appropriately, fulfilling one's **giri**, it reflects not only on the individual, but on all groups of which that individual is a part.

Situational self: Tatemae and Honne

The emphasis on harmonious relations which pervades Japanese culture can result in an apparent discrepancy between what the Japanese say and what they think. As has been mentioned previously, the maintenance of **wa** often demands subjugating one's inner feelings to the demands of the situation. **Tatemae**, one's public face, situational voice, or form, is the facade one presents in public. **Honne**, one's private face, honest voice, or substance, consists of one's true feelings that are held privately. The Bushido code has helped to institutionalise this split between real and situational self.

When individuals do not feel that they can trust others with whom they interact, they are very likely to engage in **enryo**. Generally translated to mean 'modestly holding back,' enryo refers to the hesitation which stems from not wanting to commit oneself inappropriately. In situations where a close **amae** relationship is lacking, it is not desirable to disclose one's intentions or feelings fully. To do so would be to jump prematurely into an intimate **uchi** relationship and place unfair demands on the other person. Such behaviour would signal a lack of self-restraint and be considered socially inappropriate and result in a loss of social standing. **Enryo** is manifested in such social forms as accepting something only after it has been offered three times and maintaining a generally self deprecating attitude in social relations.

COMMUNICATION

The Japanese language
The Japanese language is a reflection of society. It is highly contextual and is generally used to express respect and commonality rather than to push new ideas and individual viewpoints. To speak appropriately, one must have an intricate awareness of social relationships and be able to express them properly. Verbs are conjugated according to the degree of formality required by the situation. Words are chosen to deprecate one's accomplishments or those of one's group and to honour the accomplishments of others.

There are even separate vocabularies used for speaking to superiors, peers, or inferiors.

Communicating in English
English is a requirement in Japanese schools; most Japanese have studied English for six years by the time they leave secondary school. This does not mean, however, that everyone can speak it. Many English courses are taught by Japanese teachers whose English language skills — especially verbal — are very limited. Frequently, English-language study in Japanese schools is a case of the blind leading the blind.

Most Japanese can read and write English but have a great deal of trouble speaking it and will be nervous and embarrassed when called upon to do so. On the other hand, more and more Japanese have been travelling, studying, and working abroad in recent years, and the number of people who speak English well has greatly increased.

If you are speaking to someone who is having difficulty understanding you, try to speak slowly, avoid complicated sentences and idioms, and speak in a low voice. Unfortunately, many people think (usually unconsciously) that the way to communicate with non-English speakers is to raise their voices and say the same thing over and over again. Often this only makes the situation more uncomfortable and intimidating for the Japanese struggling to understand.

Expression of feelings

Although the Japanese do not expect all Westerners to be able to act in accordance with Japanese standards of behaviour, their sense of propriety may be affronted. Inappropriate expressions of familiarity or informality can cause discomfort, and direct expressions of disagreement tend to signal inflexibility and uncooperativeness. It is helpful to keep in mind that the Japanese rarely use the word **iie** (no) in their conversations. Instead, they express disagreement with the word **chigau** (**chigaimasu** politely), meaning 'different'.

Careful politeness and consideration for others constitute a good basis for your behaviour. Japan is a nation where individuals are generally brought up to sacrifice personal feelings and expression rather than go against group consensus. Of foremost concern to a Japanese involved in any situation are the feelings and point of view of the other person. Raising one's voice can imply a lack of self control; losing one's temper and expressing anger may well destroy a relationship. Be discreet, speak in a moderate tone of voice, and avoid loud conversations. Never call across a room, hall, or lobby and always maintain an awareness of the proper decorum for relating to other people.

In conversations you may find that responses to you are based more on people's assumptions about what you *want* to hear, than on a true reflection of the facts or underlying emotions. This is meant to be polite and kind, not an evasion or misrepresentation. Similarly, you are likely to find the topic of conversation being shifted back repeatedly to you, again as a matter of politeness and in an effort to build the all important personal bonds.

The Japanese smile is often misunderstood by Westerners. It serves a different function than in other cultures. For the Japanese, to express sorrow freely is to make the listener feel unnecessarily sad; this is considered foolish or rude or both. Theoretically, if one smiles when talking about something sad, the sorrow will be lessened a little and not passed on. In other situations, some Japanese may smile when taken to task for a fault. This does not signal contempt, insincerity, or bravado; it is an expression of embarrassment and a self-deprecating gesture.

Assumptions of agreement

The Japanese have grown up in a society where almost every single person they meet has learned to play the social games by precisely the same rules.

In such a situation, reiterations of commonly held thoughts and feelings are often unnecessary. There is no need to say something that your conversation partner already knows. Japanese communication patterns reflect this attitude. Language is used not so much to express new ideas so much as to acknowledge and reinforce the status distinctions and polite formalities so vital to a smoothly functioning society.

In countries with pluralist societies, notably the United States, people have become very reliant on what is actually said rather than on assumptions about common understandings. The less two people have in common, the more attention they will have to pay to the act of communication and the harder they must work to establish common ground.

In dealings between Japanese and Westerners, this difference in how much two individuals are assumed to have in common often produces misunderstandings. Communication styles, what is said as well as what is not said, reflect the amount of information the circumstances are expected to provide.

Individuals from Japan and from Western countries may make very different assumptions about what is being communicated and why. The amount of success such individuals will have in reducing misunderstanding will depend on their ability to clarify ideas, both by asking questions and by heeding the circumstances in which their interaction occurs.

Silence

The Japanese value silence and are comfortable with it in conversation. For the Japanese, silence is not an emptiness to be filled in; it is full of meaning in the context of the moment. Similarly, space is not the emptiness between two objects but is a substantial part of the field of observation. Japanese rock gardens often manifest this perception of space, just as traditional instrumental music incorporates the corresponding attitude towards silence.

The saying 'He who speaks does not know, he who knows does not speak' illustrates the fact that the Japanese often mistrust verbosity. They will even feign inarticulateness in their negotiations, believing it more valuable to listen than to speak. At such times nonverbal behaviour acquires even more importance, and skill at observation is much more valuable than presentation skills.

CUSTOMS AND COURTESIES

As has been stated earlier, expressing respect is very important, whether it be for age and status or for Japanese shrines and sacred places.

Familiarity with some forms of etiquette are very helpful in smoothing the way for good interaction. Small acts can be used to show respect for others: pushing in your chair when leaving a table, placing your shoes properly at the doorway, dressing neatly and keeping your shoes shined, and so on. In Japan it is important to observe and pay attention to seemingly small details. Keep in mind, however, that the key to making a good impression is an honest effort rather than a perfected result.

The bow

Bowing is the normal way in which the Japanese greet friends, pay respect, express thanks, apologise, ask favours, or say goodbye. You will see people bowing everywhere — in shops, offices, classrooms, and in the home. The depth of the bows and number of times they are repeated indicate the relationship that exists between the parties involved. The person of lower status will bow lower and stay bent longer than the person of higher status.

It is likely that most of the Japanese a Westerner meets will be accustomed to shaking hands and will do so as a gesture of courtesy even if it is not their usual practice. A bow may be combined with hand shaking; a slight bow may be more appropriate than the Western handshake. The latter is, in fact, most likely to when interacting with Japanese women. As with many areas of etiquette, observant Westerners will be able to learn by imitation.

Shoes

Shoes are removed when entering a home and places such as temples or traditional restaurants. Slippers may be provided for use inside except in **tatami** rooms (which are covered by tatami floor mats made of straw), where one walks in stockinged feet. Don't be surprised if, when you come out, you find your shoes neatly arranged, pointing outward toward the road so it will be easier for you to slip into them on leaving; this is a sign of hospitality. As a general rule, it is best to wear loafers or low-heeled slip-ons which will greatly simplify the process.

Chopsticks (ohashi)

It is not hard to learn how to eat with chopsticks, and the Japanese will take it as a compliment if you try. Generally the Japanese enjoy teaching others about their customs and would be glad to help you learn how to use chopsticks. When taking food from serving dishes, lift the food with the end that has not been in your mouth. When you are not using them, place your chopsticks side by side on the dish or propped up on a small holder if provided. Never lay your chopsticks down crossed, and never leave them standing upright stuck into food, since this is reminiscent of ceremonies connected with funerals.

Drinking rituals

Although everyday drinking customs are not performed as precisely as the tea ceremony, there are, nonetheless, very specific rules of etiquette which apply to social drinking. When two or more people drink together, it is considered bad form to allow others to pour for themselves. Every individual has a small glass or tiny **sake** cup and a large bottle of beer or flask or sake. Individuals take turns pouring for each other in an expression of selfless dedication. Since glasses are small and bottles are large, exchanges can be numerous in the course of an evening and serve to foster the interdependence so important to healthy Japanese relationships. In business settings, junior workers are sure to pour for senior workers and management and thus gain an opportunity to make informal suggestions or ask questions in an atmosphere in which improprieties may be forgiven.

Eating in public

In general, people do not eat in public. Even when buying a soft drink from one of the plentiful dispensing machines, people will generally stand next to the machine and drink the beverage completely before continuing on their way. Takeaway food is either eaten at the restaurant or taken home. At festivals and on such occasions as cherry blossom viewing, picnics are popular and eating from festival food stalls can be an exception.

Expressions of affection

Even though public touching and hugging are on the increase among younger Japanese, such public displays of affection create a bad impression when made by foreigners. Japanese individuals who are romantically involved will generally maintain a discreet distance from each other and will not even hold hands. This conservatism contrasts sharply with prevalent attitudes towards pornography and sex as reflected in print and film media.

Gift giving and favours

Many social activities in Japan are based on maintaining a balance of social obligation between individuals. As you become more and more involved in Japanese society you will become party to the system of debts and favours. The exchange of gifts exemplifies this custom.

The giving of gifts is a mark of appreciation and respect. Pupils give gifts to teachers; workers can give gifts to bosses; sometimes women give gifts to their doctors after having a baby. A printing company may give a gift to a publishing company, and a publishing company may give a gift to an author. Each of these exchanges is seen as a way of maintaining a balance between the individuals or groups involved.

The Japanese carefully monitor their 'credits and debits' and it is important for those who wish to be respected in their society to do so as well. If you do a favour for a Japanese, you will then be able to count on that person to do you a kindness. If you are given a gift, you must give one of equal value in return — favour for favour. It is important to remember that when you are initially selecting a gift, you are thereby obligating the recipient to match your gesture.

A guest always brings a gift to the host. The gift should be wrapped (most stores will wrap them for you) and presented on arrival. Do not expect your host to open it in front of you. The Japanese usually do not open gifts until after the guest has departed, since it might embarrass him or her if the gift appears to be of lesser value than appropriate.

Expressing praise and appreciation

The expression of praise can be a delicate matter in Japan. If you do not express appreciation, you might hurt someone's feelings, but if you express too much, you may in fact obligate them to give you the object of the praise or to go out of their way to accommodate your expectations in the future.

When visiting Japanese homes, you can admire flower arrangements and art objects, but not lavishly. Quiet appreciation of your surroundings is best. Many Japanese are self-conscious at having foreigners in their homes and may be very self-deprecating about what they have to offer. It is best to simply reassure them that their hospitality is very generous and that whatever is offered is more than adequate.

The Japanese are punctilious about expressing thanks for any kindness or courtesy. If you have been entertained at lunch, dinner, or afternoon tea, it is polite to thank the host or hostess, either by telephone or by note, as promptly as possible. Response time is an important element in the courtesy. Furthermore, it is customary to begin the next conversation with that person, whenever this may be, with thanks for the kindness shown on the previous occasion. This reinforces your connection with the person and the continuity of the relationship.

Japanese culture and the values that form its core have produced patterns of behaviour that differ, sometimes dramatically, from Western ones. It is impossible to cover every new custom you may encounter. In an ambiguous situation, watching to see what others do is always helpful. Being slightly hesitant and careful not only works but is generally perceived by the Japanese as respectful.

How to Live & Work in Hong Kong

A Practical Handbook for Expatriates

MARTIN BENNETT

Hong Kong continues to be one of the most dynamic commercial centres in the world, and despite the shadow over its future, it still has a thriving expatriate community. This book will be essential reading for all business and professional people and their families planning a stay in Hong Kong. Authoritative and comprehensive, it details everything you need to know about living in the colony, its future, visas and permits, money matters, accommodation, education, crime and drugs, the Chinese way of business, festivals, social nuances, and lots more vital and practical information. Martin Bennett has himself lived and worked in Hong Kong for eight years, as a Consultant in cross-cultural education and expatriate training, and lecturer at Hong Kong University.

£8.99pb, 144p illus. 1 85703 005 2. (1992)

How To Books Ltd, Plymbridge House, Estover Road, Plymouth PL6 7PZ, United Kingdom. Tel: (0752) 695745. Fax: (0752) 695699. Telex: 45635.

6
Doing Business in Japan

THE JAPANESE BUSINESS RELATIONSHIP

Westerners doing business in Japan should not be fooled by the executive dressed faultlessly in a Western business suit; underneath is a Japanese, not a Westerner. However Western his appearance and behaviour, even if he speaks fluent English, he will think Japanese.

Most Japanese, for instance, prefer to talk indirectly; 'getting to the point' is not a virtue. They prefer to ease into a subject and will go to great lengths to avoid giving a negative response, for this would cause the other person to lose face. Conversely, when they themselves receive a negative response, they feel rebuffed.

Personal introductions
The Japanese also place a high value on personal contacts and inter-mediaries. When you first meet or visit government officials or ranking businesspeople, it is very important to get a personal introduction from friends, your embassy, bank officials, or others. Direct contact without this introduction from a personal intermediary is not likely to be produc-tive. It is also important to bear in mind that the first meeting is semisocial and meant to lay the groundwork for any business exchange to follow.

How to relate to Japanese executives
Business is often initiated over long conversations accompanied by tea, sake, or a game of golf. This hospitality does not, however, indicate acceptance. It means they are feeling you out, finding your weak spots, gaining confidence in your strengths. During this process, you should show yourself at your best, that is, no familiarity, no loud boasting, no first names, no 'instant friendships'. The exact level of formality will depend on the setting. In a bar, for instance, you can behave in a more casual, relaxed manner than in a board room. The general rule is to observe

63

your Japanese counterparts closely and follow their leads. Whatever the situation, it is best not to press for decisions, official actions, or any form of commitment. The first few meetings will be a time of relationship building; serious business will be addressed later.

Conservative dress and behaviour, much bowing and smiling, and careful scrutiny of your Japanese counterpart is required on your part too. The time spent in the early stages can work to your advantage as well as theirs. Later, when you start negotiating, you will be facing tough, resilient bargainers. Just sip your tea quietly and be attentive and very polite as each of you observes the other.

The Japanese individual with whom you negotiate may in fact have little personal involvement in, or knowledge of, the issues being discussed. However, if you create a favourable impression on him, it strengthens the chances of your company being trusted, although it does not guarantee success. Fostering an atmosphere of personal respect and trust is the vital first step, a step which cannot be rushed.

Understanding the background

The current business climate in Japan is a product of centuries of strong centralised government and extremely strict and precise social patterns. Both internal and external company relationships reflect the belief that the ties of interdependency are beneficial to all involved, allowing all parties to profit from coordinated efforts. This attitude is reflected in the relationship between the megacompany and its entourage of smaller companies and the tight connections between government and industry as well as the personal relationships between supervisor and worker. The ties of commitment and dedication between Japanese companies and their employees have their roots in the strong bonds which existed historically between the samurai lords of old and their tenants. Keeping this in mind can provide insight into the psychology of the modern Japanese business-man.

To most Western executives, the firms for which they work are viewed merely as economic units, useful to them as long as they are advancing but demanding their loyalty only until something better comes along. To Japanese executives and, indeed, to all employees, a company is an interwoven community with whom they share a common destiny and for whom they willingly contribute long hours and hard work.

● The importance of this underlying difference between Western indi-
vidualism and the Japanese sense of community is impossible to
overstate.

Foreign business executives can find the tightly knit bonds of Japanese business extremely frustrating. They must fight miles of red tape simply to get their foot in the door. Westerners like to go directly to the source for products they like, but in Japan this may prove to be impossible. Often, attempts to deal directly with the intermediary channels will not only lead to dead ends but can actually be detrimental to one's intended goals. If individuals or institutions are to be successful in the Japanese business circles it is vital that they learn how those interests operate. To survive on the Japanese field of business competition, one must have a proper understanding of the rules by which the game is played.

INSIDE A JAPANESE COMPANY

The internal workings of typical Japanese companies are substantially different from those in the West. Companies recruit intensely, seeking graduates through well-respected faculty contacts at the most prestigious universities, of which Tokyo University is the leader. Contacts between veteran workers who share the new recruits' alma maters and the graduates who join the firm at the same time foster a network of relationships that binds the new recruits to the company with an emotional loyalty greater than is felt by employees anywhere else in the world. For most employees of large companies, their commitment to their employers lasts all their lives (though there are some signs that these lifetime employment patterns are beginning to change. Midcareer moves, for instance, are on the increase.)

Despite modernisation, the 'company' still remains paternalistic far beyond the levels experienced in any Western country. The larger firms often provide housing in company-owned buildings. Transport is paid for, and so is medical care. Companies provide recreation, school — even computerized marriage broking — for their young people. The employee will rarely be dropped for prolonged illness, or even inefficiency. Dismissal is likely only if the person commits a flagrant crime or violates one of the company's rules. With job security like this, one can understand why employees rarely quit to find anything better. The departing employees may find that other large Japanese companies hesitate to hire them, and if an employee does enter a new firm, previous experience may be disregarded. It may even be necessary to start again at the bottom of the pay scale.

The company as family

Some time back a picture on the front page of the *Japan Times* showed ten august, elderly directors of a large company standing with hands joined in a circle around an electric turbine on which sprays of flowers had been placed. They were 'retiring' the turbine after years of faithful service. This kind of concern for and personalisation of even their mechanical equipment reflects the degree to which employees identify with their company.

The structure of the Japanese company tends to reflect an extended family and is generally run according to Confucian ethics of morality. Rank is determined by seniority rather than merit, with positions of power invariably inherited by the 'eldest son'; many cousin companies will interact as one family; and a proud heritage may be carefully guarded.

The connection between individual and company is manifested in various ways not shared by Western workers and employers, such as company songs sung in unison at the start of each working day. Westerners simply do not make the effort to foster the same depth of loyalty and love for their companies, for fellow workers, for the product, or for the plant that the Japanese do. The Japanese miss in their Western business associates that kind of concern for the workforce and team play.

Nenko Joretsu

As mentioned above, loyalty is rewarded through a promotional system based largely on seniority. This system is known as **nenko joretsu**, and it is a key feature of the Japanese business world. In all companies there is an established pecking order, and despite a certain amount of normal jockeying for position, most employees accept their own ranking. In time, given at least minimum abilities and reasonably well-cultivated personal relationships within the company, they will move up, often as the protégé of the individual who has vacated his own post in climbing the company ladder. Promotions sometimes occur in blocks. It is rare for an individual to move up out of turn, no matter how highly supervisors regard his talents.

Great stress is laid on the team concept. One performs one's duties for the good of the whole: the company, the division, one's own tiny subsection. One relies on one's subordinates and superiors and is relied upon in the same way. It is only within this context of proven trust that individual ambition is nurtured and, in the company's own good time, rewarded.

Ringi Seido

It is through this closely knit and interlocking network of personnel ranging from top management down to the rank and file that decisions are processed, amended, and finally implemented. Thus, it is essential for the foreign businessperson in Japan to acquire some understanding of how the process works.

Ringi Seido is the corporate version of government by consensus. Decisions are not simply handed down, they are proposed and aired in sometimes endless conferences at all levels of the company even when final confirmation is a foregone conclusion. The process may take weeks, months, or even years, but by the time the decision is finally implemented, not only have all relevant staff members participated in the process, they have pretty well mastered the *what, when* and *how* of their own responsibilities in the project. As veteran foreign businesspeople in Japan are quick to point out, it may take the Japanese a small eternity to arrive at a conclusion, but having reached it, they are swift and sure about putting it into practice.

Another important feature of **ringi seido** is that is allows even those on the lower echelons to come forward with projects and proposals of their own. Indeed, such rank-and-file initiative is encouraged. The Japanese themselves like to call it 'decision making from the bottom up'. In practice, it is something less than that, but the idea of creating a consensus that draws on the whole hierarchy lies at the heart of Japanese business philosophy and methods.

Nemawashi

An aspect of business in Japan which is often overlooked by outsiders involves the Japanese style of seeking information consensus on ideas before they are formally presented to management. This process is called **nemawashi**. It involves indirect discussion and exploration of the attitudes and opinions of the powerful parties concerned before any concrete steps are taken in any direction.

Nemawashi works to maintain harmony between individuals because it eliminates the need for anyone to risk presenting new ideas that may not be acceptable to others. Any conflict that may arise during **nemawashi** can be settled in a subtle way not possible once a situation has entered the formal protocol-driven bureaucracy. **Nemawashi** is generally practised in the social arena in which any mistaken comments can be forgiven as by-products of a little too much to drink. For this reason social times are much more important to the smooth working of Japanese business and integral to managerial life than Westerners usually realise.

The time factor

Even when you are dealing with top management, business relationships often take a long time to develop. You may have had a very successful negotiation and a clear agreement in principle, but you may have to wait weeks or longer for anything to come of it. Frustrating as this can be, there is little you can do about it. The wheels are turning inexorably as they must, and you do your cause more harm than good by trying to hurry the process.

Rarely will you get quick action 'unless,' as one veteran of the business wars puts is, 'you've got gold that's worth $1.50 on the open market to sell for $1.25. Then you'll get action without delay.' In fact, you may sometimes encounter Japanese businessmen who will make concessions to Western impatience and actually shorten their normal deliberations, but don't count on it. If you were to survey a pool of successful foreign business executives in Japan, asking them for the single personal attribute that has contributed most to their own success, the overwhelming answer would surely be 'patience'.

The other side of this coin is that if the Japanese decide against the proposed relationship, it may be difficult to find out since they are, in general, reluctant to say no directly. Determining whether the Japanese are engaged in slow deliberations or avoiding a forthright rejection will demand careful attention to the process of communication, careful examination of the behaviour of those involved, and weighing up what has not been done or said as well as what has. Several vague statements about the prospects of a relationship accompanied by an absence of action may signal a no.

Harmony in business relationships

One of the most subtle but important considerations, as noted earlier in chapter 5, relates to **wa**. This can be defined as 'harmony', a comfortable atmosphere of acceptance and respect. **Wa** avoids abruptness or lack of sensitivity to people's feelings. These 'disharmonies' are contrary to the Japanese sense of decorum. Japanese people often feel that Westerners operate by the law and the book, without this all-important sense of personal connection, without **wa**. We cannot exaggerate the importance of maintaining a harmonious atmosphere. Take special care never to embarrass your Japanese counterparts or to act, even inadvertently, in ways that might cause them to feel embarrassed, ashamed, or subject to blame. while this care should be taken in any business dealings anywhere in the world, it especially important in Japan, where an inadvertent slip might lead to loss of trust which has taken long to develop. The result can be a serious deterioration of your business dealings for apparently no reason.

Women in the workplace

In Japanese international corporations in Japan women are almost invariably denied access to managerial positions. With an educational system which encourages girls to compete on an equal footing with boys, it is often surprising to Westerners that Japanese big business does not seem to take full advantage of the university resource pools.

Compared with most Western countries, a large proportion of working women in Japan, as many as one out of five, are non-wage earners in small, family-owned businesses. Women who join the corporate world are almost exclusively employed as secretaries and coffee and tea servers and are called 'office ladies'. As is invariably pointed out, this is because they are perceived as temporary workers who will leave the company soon after marriage.

In large companies the seniority systems reflect the Confucian ethic that women in their youth should obey their father, in their maturity their husband, and in old age their son. Little room exists for the idea of women as managers or even as senior personnel. In areas less heavily bound by conservative tradition, women are better able to make their mark and even excel. Small and middle-sized companies are very likely to have female managers or even presidents and owners, especially in fields considered more 'feminine', such as cosmetic industries and real estate.

Today, it is becoming evident that Japan is changing. In recent years women have become a visible minority in business and government, making up about six percent of management in large corporations and holding several key positions in government such as the leadership of the Socialist party. In shifting economic times it has become necessary for married women to join the workforce again when children are old enough. Circumstances have made it clear that a second income is vital for the financial security of the Japanese family. It will take time for women to gain a true voice in the ranks of Japan's male-dominated economic leadership, but the trend has certainly begun.

The number of expatriate women involved in big business in Japan is also on the rise. Gradually more Western women are becoming primary wage earners or remaining unmarried as they climb their career ladders. The result is that there are more businesswomen being assigned to Japanese posts.

Realisations about women's effectiveness are replacing myths that expatriate women would necessarily be at a disadvantage in a male-oriented Japanese business world. True, expatriate women will probably have to work harder than men to build a relationship with their Japanese counterparts, but feelings of uncertainty about how to interact with the foreign businesswoman are more likely to be the cause rather than the existence of prejudices about capabilities.

How to build relationships

How can you as a Western manager project greater warmth and foster the atmosphere of personal respect and trust that the Japanese value? by emphasising personal relationships more than you normally would. Walk through the plant or office often, greet people by name, talk to workers and — even more important — listen to them. Appear at sports and other social events in which colleagues and workers participate. Be ready to spend evenings out with your associates, cementing personal bonds and practising **nemawashi**. Executives regularly take their juniors out for evenings of food and drink, which helps to melt the barriers that build up during working hours and allow informal exchange of ideas and opinions. Junior executives also go out with equals as well as superiors so as to form a bond supplemental to that of the workplace.

● One simple piece of advice to Western managers newly arrived in Japan is this: as soon as possible after your arrival, budget into your work week an ample number of hours for socialising, not only with your Japanese counterpart but also up and down the executive line. Establish yourself quickly as a personable individual and a team player. It is important to keep in regular touch with people lower as well as higher in the organisation. Westerners normally think of themselves as friendly people but do not always appear so as they sit in their offices, sending memos and faxes, making calls, and perhaps making announcements over a public address system. Try to communicate about substantive issue on a face-to-face basis, even if it is actually through a representative or an intermediary. This is far more effective than written or telephone communication and serves to engender personal warmth.

CONTRACTS, THE LAW, AND TRADITION

The Japanese say 'Westerners try to negotiate a contract; the Japanese try to negotiate a relationship.' Westerners feel that an agreement in writing is the way to avoid or deal with problems. The Japanese feel a continuing dynamic relationship is the way to solve problems. So, as you talk and work together, they are trying to get to know you while you are trying to finalise points leading to the culmination of a deal. Furthermore, once you do reach agreement, it is important to realise that both sides have very different attitudes about the interpretation of that agreement and about resolving disputes that may arise.

Because the Japanese are thinking in terms of relationships, they are quick to ask for a change in terms if conditions change; the fact that it was a hard-bargained contract and has been jointly signed is not significant to them. Westerners, who think 'contract' and 'moral obligation' are synonymous, are jolted by the idea.

In terms of Western law, one side cannot force a change because outside circumstances change. But in Japan traditional values rather than legal considerations are what dictate action. Law is a Western import based almost entirely on American and European models. Many laws were actually imposed on the Japanese during the American Occupation, and so feel less comfortable to the Japanese than more traditional concepts, which are often not in harmony with the legal code. This can create problems for Westerners who operate on such different principles and are unfamiliar with traditional Japanese attitudes.

- The Japanese rarely use lawyers or courts; to them the whole concept is confrontational and best avoided.

Until the later part of the last century, whenever disputes were made public, both parties were severely punished regardless of guilt or innocence. Maintenance of the appearance of harmony was most important. What went on beneath the surface did not matter. Today, law is more like a ceremonial sword; it is meant to be brandished but not used to kill. They greatly prefer mediation or, if necessary, may turn to the government to intercede and fulfill its 'duty', which is to look after those in its care.

This makes for an interdependence between government and business that works well for the Japanese. A system explicitly based on individual rights is unnecessary. Scholarly opinion and old and respected views are often called in to take the place of a legal confrontation. There are, in fact, very few lawyers in Japan. Justice is far more apt to be judge-oriented than lawyer-oriented because judges are more interested in seeking out the truth than are competing lawyers. This concept fits Japan's paternalistic outlook better than an adversarial system. Out-of-court conciliation is preferred. The harmony and stability of the group involved take precedence over nearly all disagreements. Failure to compromise is not seen as strength in Japan but as weakness, which may result in an embarrassing loss of face.

With this in mind, it becomes easier to understand why the Japanese avoid categorical statements and allow for leeway in their business dealings. As has been mentioned elsewhere, the Japanese rarely give an unqualified 'no'; in fact, they often say yes when they mean no. It is, therefore, important for Westerners to watch for and learn to read negative signs in a response: hesitancy in speech, questioning expressions, a slight hiss between the teeth as the head is cocked to one side, an unwillingness to be specific, delaying phrases like 'it will take a little bit more time'. Part of the Japanese distrust of contracts is that written instruments don't allow the flexibility and leeway they feel they need in order to adapt to changing conditions.

In general, written documents are not considered adequate for establishing a sound relationship or even for communicating effectively. You may find that your first exploratory letters go unanswered for a number of possible reasons. Perhaps you did not include enough information in them but they would not want to embarrass you by saying so. Perhaps, if it is a small or medium-sized firm, they cannot reply in English. (Have your letters translated into Japanese if you can; they will then feel free to respond in Japanese.) Finally, sometimes decision making is so dispersed that the company cannot give you an answer. But generally, the Japanese simply prefer face-to-face contact. Not receiving a written answer should not be taken as an insult or a brush-off. Just try again, but in person or through an intermediary.

HOW TO USE INTERPRETERS

Language is often a major cause for delay in business dealings. Even in big companies, any non-Japanese written matter is channelled through a translating staff that is usually small and often overworked. This, compounded by the fact that even minor decisions must receive the stamp of senior management, means that Western patience is often tried to the extreme.

It is advisable, as well as courteous, to take your interpreter to all business meetings. Although younger executives often speak English, especially if they function at the top levels, you cannot assume this will be the case. Older Japanese often do not speak English well, and English is spoken less and less as you get into line operations. Furthermore, you want to be sure than *you* understand all the nuances of what is being said. If you develop a good relationship with an interpreter, she or he can be extremely helpful in steering you past many of the pitfalls of your Japanese business relationships.

BUSINESS CUSTOMS

Business entertaining
Since personal interaction is crucial at all stages of a business relationship,

the almost endless entertaining does not stop when a deal is consummated. Unless you are the **Nan-ba-wan** (Number One Man), top Japanese executives are likely to bow out when the negotiation is completed and middle management takes over. Then you start all over again. They, too, like to go out on the town, and play golf.

Japanese men traditionally let their hair down in the informal atmosphere of restaurants and inns during what some Westerners feel is an excessive amount of mutual entertaining, usually of a pretty lavish nature. Executives above the managerial level (**kacho**) are known in the entertainment trades as **shayo-zoku,** or the 'expense-account class'. Department heads often like to entertain their subordinates in order to keep interpersonal frictions to a minimum and to ensure loyalty; all these various expense account spenders keep thousands of plush bars, cabarets, restaurants, and inns full and profitable. However, since many men go out several evenings a week, they normally retire early. Evenings end about 11.00 pm. There are a few all-night and 'after hours' spots, but most are dark and quiet by midnight.

Basically, there are three types of drinking places in Japan that serve alcoholic beverages.

1. Cabarets
A cabaret is a bar or hostess bar in which a hostess is automatically assigned to each guest as soon as he comes in, and titbits such as peanuts are served automatically, often with beer. After the first 'set', drinks are ordered separately. Hostesses' fees are usually included in the overall cost.

2. Night clubs
Night clubs are much the same as cabarets except that there is a cover charge, food and drink are served only when ordered, and the customer asks for a hostess if he wants one. Both cabarets and night clubs have dancing (and often floor shows) and are required by law to close at 11.30 pm.

3. General drinking places
Bars that are not licensed to employ hostesses or serve food may legally stay open until midnight. To stay open after midnight, a night spot must serve food and be classed as a 'restaurant' (which is why so many of the most popular cabarets and night clubs double as restaurants). Most of these places add a 10-15 percent service charge, plus another 10-15 percent entertainment tax.

A word of caution
Western businessmen sometimes get 'taken' at unscrupulous cabarets, where several 'hostesses' join the table without being invited and deliberately run the bill up to astronomical figures. The best way to avoid this, of course, is to go with a Japanese colleague. The good places tend to be very expensive by international standards since most customers are on liberal company expense accounts and do not worry about the cost.

Gift giving
Businessmen in Japan who give parties for their associates or clients usually provide a gift for each guest — anything from an attractive hand towel to a fairly expensive piece of lacquerware. Just before returning home, you should give token gifts to anyone who was especially helpful. If you give a gift to a top-ranking person, it must be something of value; otherwise it might be taken as an insincere gesture. Pay attention to gifts that you receive and that others give to their superiors. This is a very good way to learn how much it is appropriate to spend. Good scotch and cognac are expensive and universally appreciated. The smart traveller brings these in from duty-free shops en route and uses them for special gifts. (Three bottles are allowed tax-free.) Items that you can have personalised such as golfballs or items bearing company logos are also good choices.

Business cards
Business cars (**meishi**) are essential, both as a courtesy and to help you keep difficult names straight. The exchange of cards is vital for the Japanese as it quickly enables them to determine the rank of each person involved and to respond accordingly.

●   When you are introduced to more than one person at a time, take care to give your card to the senior man first. Not to do so is a severe breach of etiquette. The Japanese will gloss over your slight, but it is definitely to your advantage to do it right. You will understand clearly who the boss is by the respectful attitudes expressed by those around him.

There is a story of one American who took everyone's card, then sat down and rummaged through his briefcase until he found his own, whereupon he flipped them casually around the circle as if he were dealing cards. He never got to first base; his behaviour was considered mocking and insulting. Less obviously disrespectful behaviour such as making a note on a card or failing to give it adequate attention can be nearly as distressing to the Japanese.

You don't give your cards to everyone you meet, but it is polite to return the courtesy if the other person gives you a card, and you should be prepared to offer yours to anyone whose name you want to remember. Be sure to have some made in advance (at least a hundred), with the information printed in Japanese on one side and English on the other.

Cards should be handed to the other person with both hands and right side up so that the receiver can read the correct print without having to turn the card at all. When you are given someone's card, it must be accepted with due respect. Do not just stuff it in your pocket. Look carefully at the card and handle it as if it were a gift, expressing your thanks and appreciation. Later, when you are alone, you can write a note on it for future reference. If you handle a business card casually, you will present a poor image of yourself and your company.

BUSINESS MECHANICS

Working hours

Japanese businesses are gradually changing to the five-day week. In practice, however, many lower- and mid-level executives, known as 'salarymen', work twelve hours a day six days a week.

Normal working hours in Japan

Banks
9.00am to 6.00pm, weekdays. Cash card services are available during normal working hours.

Post Offices
9.00am to 5.00pm weekdays. Main branches are also open from 9.00am to 2.00pm on Saturdays.

Government offices
9.00am to 5.00pm, weekdays.

Department stores
usually closed one day a week (most often Monday).

Holidays

There are many Japanese holidays, and below is a list of the official ones. Note that Christmas Day is *not* an official holiday in Japan. Offices will be open and doing business. New Year, however, lasts a week or more. Many banks and other firms close down from 28th December to 4th January and also during August for **Obon**.

Public holidays in Japan

New Year Holiday	January 1-3
Adult's Day	January 15
National Foundation Day	February 11
Vernal Equinox Day	March 21 or 22
Green Day	April 29
Constitution Day	May 3
Citizens' Day	May 4
Children's Day	May 5
Respect for the Aged Day	September 15
Autumnal Equinox Day	September 23 or 24
Sports Day	October 10
Cultural Day	November 3
Labour-Thanksgiving Day	November 23
Emperor's Birthday	December 23

The Japanese tend to take their vacations during the following periods, usually not for more than a week at a time:

- New year (**Oshogatsu**)   end of December to January 10
- Golden Week   end of April to early May
- **Obon** Holiday   middle of August

At these times it is especially important to make advance train, hotel, and restaurant reservations. All facilities and transport services are crowded.

BUSINESS HOTELS

Most visiting executives stay at first-class hotels like the Imperial and the

Okura. As an alternative there are 'business hotels' noted for their economical and practical service; they are especially suited for single travellers and small groups. Most of the rooms are singles. There are no baggage porter services, and there is no room service, although it may be possible to eat meals in a common room with other guests.

● Write to the **Japan Business Hotel Association**, 3 Kanda Higashi-Matsushita-cho, Chiyoda-ku, Tokyo. Tel: (03) 258-1090. The Association has listings of over four hundred business hotels throughout Japan.

VISITING JAPANESE COMPANIES

Many Japanese companies have conducted tours through their factories where you can see their operations firsthand. It can be valuable experience for anyone interested in Japanese production methods (for details see Chapter 12, **Cities**).

7
Daily Living for Expatriates

HOUSING

Finding a house

Housing in Japan can be extremely difficult to find. As a buyer in a seller's market, you will be fighting a large demand for rented accommodation. Since you will automatically be at a disadvantage as a newcomer, you will need some assistance. Landlords often do not speak English and all documents will be in Japanese. The best help, therefore, would be someone who is bilingual.

Often companies will help relocated employees find housing, but if yours does not, you may want to try **International Business Representatives** in Tokyo, an organisation that can render valuable assistance to foreigners just settling in to Japan. Your embassy should be able to direct you to other useful relocation services.

When you begin your search, be prepared to encounter rents that will seem sky high by Western standards. The rental policies which landlords adhere to can also seem a bit demanding. Depending on the landlord, you may be asked to put down a deposit, or **shikikin**, the refund of which is contingent upon satisfactory return of the property to its original state. You may also have to pay a nonrefundable service fee (**reikin**) which may amount to as much as several months' rent. For instance, a Japanese student leasing a Y50,000 per month apartment in Tokyo paid two months' rent (Y100,000) in advance, a **shikikin** equal to two months' rent and another two months' rent as **reikin**, totalling Y300,000. The amount of **shikikin** he gets back will depend on how much work the apartment needs when he leaves, which is at the discretion of the landlord.

A tradition of uchi

For the Japanese there is a strong delineation between the inside of a house, **uchi**, and the outside, **soto**. Although dense population conditions demand that living spaces be very limited in size (averaging about 750 square feet per household), domestic simplicity and bareness serve to counter balance the frenzy of metropolitan streets. Outside the home an individual must fight the crowds and advances of a technological age, but inside the **uchi** peaceful order reflects the Japanese view of inner harmony.

Japanese-style homes

Japanese houses are traditionally built to maximize ventilation during the hot and muggy summer months. As a result, buildings are light and airy, designed for simplicity and utility. To take advantage of any slight breeze they are often raised above the ground to allow for maximum circulation of air. Traditional homes are wood framed, generally with moveable side panels acting as walls or screens between rooms. There are two types of screens: the **fusuma** and the **shoji**. The fusuma is a panel of heavy paper stretched over a wood frame, pairs of which generally serve as doors for rooms or closets in which bedding and other items are stored. The shoji is a screen covered by thin translucent paper which may act as a sliding door or partition between rooms.

Floors are covered by rice straw mats encased in tightly woven rushes. These are called **tatami** mats and are found in all Japanese rooms. There is usually very little furniture, and what there is will be multipurpose, easy to move, and close to the floor. Shoes are never worn in the tatami floors, and the tradition of removing one's shoes at the door persists today even in the carpeted rooms of Western-style homes.

Western-style homes

Modern houses are often a mix of traditional and Euro-American styles. Modern houses may be completely modernised, with wall-to-wall carpeting, central heating, and a full range of the latest energy-saving appliances. It is more likely however, that there will be at least one **tatami** room and no central heating. If there is no central heating a **kotatsu** will invariably be present in commonly used rooms. Before the advent of electricity, the **kotatsu** was generally a deep hole in the floor beneath the central table in which hot coals would be placed. Today's incarnation is more likely to be a table with electric coils in its underside and a heavy quiltlike skirt that is placed across one's lap. Other alternatives for those cold winter months include kerosene, propane, or electric heaters.

Most Japanese sleep on quilt-like mats called **futons**, a duvet-style furnishing familiar to many Westerners, although the western variety is usually thicker and heavier than that found in Japan. Futons are spread on the floor at night and rolled up or folded and stored in the closet during the day.

The Japanese bath is called the **ofuro**. The tub is much deeper and shorter than those generally found in the West. Since the size demands the use of so much water, the ofuro will usually be filled just once for an evening of bathing in which the whole family takes turns. To keep the water clean, one washes and rinses completely before getting into the bath. The water is kept very hot throughout by an independent heating system. The ofuro is a treat of Japanese civilization which should not be missed.

Although most houses have an ofuro it is possible to find homes that do not yet have a flush toilet, especially in older residential areas away from large cities. It is a sign of the paradoxical development of Japan that homes lacking in flush toilets may have the latest in computer technology and video equipment.

You will often encounter the old-style toilets — which you stand or squat over rather than sit on. In most public conveniences such as those found in theatres, stations, and so forth, you will find at least one or two Western toilets.

FURNISHINGS, APPLIANCES, AND ELECTRICITY

It is difficult to give advice on furnishing your home because tastes vary. Some people are much happier when surrounded by their own furniture; others prefer not to risk shipping.

If you plan to take your own furniture, ship only the things you can't live without. Leave large items behind. Assuming you can get them through the door, large sofas, overstuffed chairs, and heavy sideboards look peculiar in small Japanese-style houses and apartments. Take smaller items, but bear in mind that you may have fewer and/or smaller rooms than at home and that the preference in Japan is for sparsely furnished, uncluttered space.

You may want to consider buying new appliances in Japan; they are high-quality and servicing is reliable and free within the guarantee period. If you are happy with used appliances, you can often pick up excellent buys from departing foreigners or from used appliance shops. Used appliances and furniture are often advertised in the *Tokyo Weekender*, a local English-language weekly, or at the American Club.

Apartment houses may or may not furnish washers and dryers either in the apartment, in the basement, or on the roof. Dehumidifiers are useful and are usually supplied in Western-style apartments but not in houses. Cookers and refrigerators may also be supplied in rented apartments, depending on the landlords. Most cookers use gas rather than electricity, and due to limited kitchen space, ovens are the exception rather than the rule. In general the availability of appliances must be explored carefully.

Electrical current in most of eastern Japan, including Tokyo, is AC 100 volts, 50 cycles. The service is dependable though expensive. In western Japan (divided about halfway between Tokyo and Nagoya and including Osaka) current is 60 cycles. Anything made for 110 volts, 50/60 cycles will probably work satisfactorily, but radios, record players, and tape recorders may run slower than normal. Houses tend to have fewer electrical outlets and less electrical wiring than those in other industrialised countries.

TELEPHONES

Telephones are obtained from the Nippon Telegraph and Telephone Company, and phone service is usually good. Installation generally takes a week to a month, or even longer depending on circumstances. You are required to purchase a deposit bond of about Y70,000 to 90,000 and to pay an installation fee. The bond is refundable after ten years, or it can be sold — as is done in most cases — to the next tenant or on the open market. In order to expedite the whole process, some people use a middleman or telephone broker.

● Rates are much higher on calls made from Japan to other countries compared with the incoming calls from abroad. Thus, you may want to arrange to have your family or your home office phone you instead.

HOW TO FIND DOMESTIC HELP

At one time everyone had help in Japan, but those days have gone. As in many countries, most people prefer industrial and commercial jobs to domestic services, and prices for help are soaring. A live-in maid who does not cook can charge as much as Y100,000 a month.

Some large families have one all-purpose maid who cooks, cleans, and does the laundry. Most foreigners, however, do their own shopping and cooking, possibly having some help with cleaning. There are laundromats and laundries available if your home or apartment building doesn't provide washers and dryers.

Babysitting services are available in all the big cities, but they tend to be expensive, inconvenient, and the sitters lacking in English skills. Enlisting services can be time consuming and can require a great deal of advance notice. Live-in students can sometimes be found to help with children.

● The **Tokyo Domestic Service Centre** provides English-speaking maids and babysitters. Tel: (03) 584-4769.

SHOPPING

Fish, meat, and poultry
Fish is Japan's staple food. The variety is enormous, plentiful, of high quality, and available at a reasonable cost, though prices have been on the up as a result of international fishing laws. Some varieties will be familiar but there will be ample opportunity to experiment with new kinds of fish.

Ham and pork are plentiful. Beef is available and of good quality but very expensive, since most of it is imported. Chickens are often small and thin but can be bought ground, boned, cubed, or prepared in other ways.

Frozen and canned foods
Imported frozen and canned foods will cost double or more what you pay at home. Japanese brands are of very good quality, and more and more foods are being labelled in English as well as Japanese.

Fruit
Generally, fruit is bought only when in season. Some fruits will look familiar; many others may be new to you. There is a mandarin orange, called **mikan**, which is extremely good, quite cheap, and available from autumn to spring. **Nashi** is a fruit having the consistency of an apple and the taste of a pear. It is sometimes called an Asian pear and is now exported to the West. Persimmons are plentiful and delicious in autumn. Kiwis, bananas, strawberries, grapes and apples are plentiful yet expensive out of season. Melons are exceedingly expensive at any time and seen as highly valued gift items.

Other products
Japanese cigarettes are strong, though mild ones are available. Mild Seven Select is the most popular brand, followed by Seven Stars and its milder version, Mild Seven. Western pharmaceuticals such as Colgate tooth-paste, Bayer aspirin, Johnson & Johnson shampoo and similar products are readily available, but local brands are comparable and of course cheaper. Imported wines and spirits are more expensive than in many other countries. Japanese Suntory whisky is extremely popular in Japan.

Local clubs and nightspots often keep personalised bottles for regular customers. Beer has almost replaced sake as the national drink and is available in many high-quality Japanese brands.

Specialised neighbourhood stores may have lower prices than the large, more convenient supermarkets or the basement food sections of the major department stores, which have English-speaking clerks. Kinokuniya, Natimal and Azabu supermarkets offer charge accounts and accept orders by telephone. Other large shops in Tokyo where English is spoken and foreign tastes are catered to are Meidi-ya, Olympia Foodliner, and Hara Store.

Beauty salons

When looking for a beauty salon it is usually best, initially, to go to those in the major hotels because the hairdressers are used to Western hair; they also speak English. There are, of course, other first-class shops as well, but it takes a little time to find them.

Department stores

Some of the main department stores are:

Matsuya	Seibu
Marui	Sogo
Mitsukoshi	Matsuzakaya
Isetan	Takashimaya

Large stores are open from 10.00am to 6.00pm. There are many excellent small shops, too, which are often open until 10.00pm. Department stores each close one day a week but not all on the same day and never on Sunday — the biggest shopping day.

Shopping can be a pleasure in Japan. Salespeople are professionals dedicated to their jobs and a great deal of care is taken to satisfy the customer's needs. Packages are always carefully and beautifully wrapped and delivered to the customer with an efficiency rarely matched in other countries. Some shops may deliver even small articles to your home.

It is generally best to be prepared to pay in cash. International credit cards can be used in most large department stores, hotels, and restaurants but not in smaller shops. Only the larger stores have their own charge cards. If you have one of these cards, don't lose it; cancelling it may take as much as a month. As stated before, personal cheques are not used in Japan.

When you enter Japan, be sure to get a form from the Customs Office called **Record of Purchases of Commodities Tax Exempt for Export**. Take it with you whenever you make a major purchase and have it marked by the salesperson; otherwise, you may have to pay heavily on your departure.

ROLE OF A NON-WORKING SPOUSE

Whenever a couple moves to a new country to set up home, both individuals will go through a period of adjustment to their new surroundings. In relationships where one partner is working and the other is not, the demands placed on each will very different. It is important to recognise this and the fact that both individuals will have to adapt to new environments in distinct and dissimilar ways.

Typically more men than women are asked to take on foreign assignments. This means that most non-working expatriates in Japan are wives of businessmen. They are especially likely to feel all the differences between their home countries and Japan. Since they are not as likely to be in the more or less universal activities of the business world, wives must develop different coping strategies and learn about a different side of Japanese culture.

In post war Japan it became a sign of affluence for wives to leave the workforce upon marriage or soon afterwards. Initially only wealthy businessmen could afford to support a non-working wife but as many Japanese increased their earning power it became a status symbol of the middle class. The Japanese wife was expected to dedicate herself to the home and children while the husband was expected to devote himself to his company. The relationship between husband and wife was secondary to their respective duties.

For many non-Japanese couples this is hard to accept. The extent to which husbands' and wives' lives overlap is in large part culturally determined. By Japanese tradition, wives rarely accompany their husbands on business social occasions. 'The Japanese wife is obliged to obey that custom,' said one executive. 'She is used to the system.' Wives of foreign businessmen, however, may initially find the expectations of the Japanese system rather disagreeable. 'They know it is the custom but they resent it,' said an executive of Scott Paper in Tokyo. 'Some never accept the fact that Japan is a man's world.'

One of the wives advises, 'You have to have a sense of humour. Sometimes, actually, I would rather be at home than grinding around that same old golf course again, being so polite. However, you do learn to read each invitation carefully to see if you are included, for when you are, you are expected to go.'

With a few formal obligations in the business world, the non-working spouse can learn about Japan by taking advantage of the many opportunities for active involvement in organisations and associations. There are school PTA meetings, bridge games and churches to attend. The various national clubs are centres for many activities. For instance, members of the **Tokyo Women's Club** (which requires a small fee and introduction by a member) are eligible for its courses, outings, and speaker luncheons — all providing opportunities to meet new people, both Japanese and foreign.

If you have had at least one year of college, or university the **College Women's Association** provides a wealth of activities too, with a chance to meet a large and internationally diverse groups of members. This club sponsors a yearly lecture series, various kinds of study groups, an annual exhibition and sale of Japanese prints, and travel programmes.

Volunteer opportunities include teaching English in one of the many English-language schools, or helping to prepare Japanese business wives going abroad for the first time. The **International Ladies' Benevolent Society**, which meets every month at different embassies, helps various Japanese charities. It too requires an introduction to join.

There are countless opportunities to learn about Japan's unique and fascinating culture and to become engaged in worthwhile activities.

FOREIGN RESIDENTS ADVISORY CENTRES

The Foreign Residents' Advisory Centres offer advice in English on questions about housing, paying bills, and most other matters that foreigners need help with when living in Japan.

Tokyo	Tel:	(03)	211-4433
Chiba prefecture	Tel:	(0472)	23-2414
Kanagawa prefecture	Tel:	(045)	324-2299
Saitama prefecture	Tel:	(048)	647-4175
Fukuoka	Tel:	(092)	733-2220

8
Health and
Medical Care

PUBLIC HEALTH

Japanese and Western health standards are comparable, except that the Japanese express very much more concern about spreading disease from one person to another. Many Japanese wear white gauze face masks when suffering from colds or flu to protect others from their germs. Even with these precautions, though, the common cold in this heavily populated country runs rampant during the winter season. During the humid summer season, air pollution can be a problem in urban areas. At its worst, smog in the Tokyo/Yokohama and Osaka areas can cause breathing difficulties, especially for people with a history of respiratory problems.

In Tokyo and other major cities, food and drink are generally up to the best standards. Tap water is safe to drink, but it contains no fluoride. Commercial milk products are safe.

The famous Japanese 'hot baths' should be avoided by anyone with high blood pressure. If you ever become overheated, follow the same treatment as for heat prostration: recline with the head higher than the rest of the body and do everything possible (with cold water and ice) to cool the skin quickly.

MEDICAL CARE

Immunisations are not required for entry into Japan; nonetheless, it is a good idea for any traveller to keep all inoculations up to date, especially for diphtheria, tetanus, typhoid, and paratyphoid. It is also important to bring all your medical and dental records.

Always carry a medical record card, which is written in both English and Japanese and lists your name, age, blood group, and drug allergies. You can obtain one free of charge for each member of your family from the American Chamber of Commerce in Tokyo, 7F Fukide Daini Building, 4-1-4 Torano Minato-ku 105, tel: (03) 433-5381. The card comes in a plastic case which can also be used to hold your alien registration card. Specify the number of cards you wish to have and remember to give your full address.

Doctors and hospitals are generally excellent, and there are many private clinics, the best of which are in the large, well-known Japanese hospitals. A number of Japanese practitioners speak English, and many are trained in North America or Europe. People come to Japan from other parts of Asia for the excellent medical care and clean and well-equipped hospitals.

The system for providing medical care differs somewhat from that of other countries. The procedure at hospitals and doctors' offices in Japan is like that of a public clinic where people queue to see the doctor without first making an appointment. All medicines are dispensed by the hospital, and there tends to be a heavy reliance on drugs as the preferred treatment for most ailments. All bills are settled on the day of service before the patient leaves the hospital, so those with foreign insurance will have to look for reimbursement later.

Because of the deference the Japanese show to rank and position, Japanese doctors receive a great deal of respect. Japanese patients implicitly trust their doctors to the extent that doctors may not automatically report all information about patients' conditions. This is in sharp contrast to the Euro-American tradition of fully informing patients of their conditions.

● Find a doctor soon after your arrival and familiarise yourself with how the medical/emergency system works — *before* you need it.

Your company or organisation may recommend specific doctors and/or hospitals with English-speaking staff. We have included a partial listing below; for further information, contact either the Japan Tourist Organization (JNTO) or your embassy for their lists.

CLINICS AND HOSPITALS

General medical clinics

● Bluff Clinic, 82 Yamate-cho Naka-ku, Yokohama. Tel: (0456) 41-6961.

● Hibiya Clinic, B1F Mitsui Building, 1-1-2 Yurakucho, Chiyoda-ku, Tokyo. Tel: (03) 520-2681.

● Imperial Clinic, 4F Imperial Hotel, 1-1-1 Uchisaiwacho, Chiyoda-ku, Tokyo. Tel: (03) 503-8681.

● International Clinic, 1-5-9 Azabudai Minato-ku, Tokyo. Tel: (03) 582-2624.

● National Medical Clinic, 5F National Azabu Supermarket Building, 4-5-2 Minami Azabu Minato-ku, Tokyo.

● Tokyo Medical and Surgical Clinic, 2F Mori Building, 3-4-30 Shiba Koen Minato-ku, Tokyo. Tel: (03) 436-3028.

Hospitals in the Tokyo area

● International Catholic Hospital (**Seibo Byoin**), 2-5-1 Naka-Ochiai Shinjuku-ku, Tokyo. Tel: (03) 951-1111.

● St Luke's International Hospital, 10-1 Akashicho Chuo-ku, Tokyo. Tel: (03) 541-5151.

● Tokyo Adventist Hospital (**Aisei Byoin**), 3-17-3 Amanuma Sugina-mi-ku, Tokyo. Tel: (03) 392-6151.

Hospitals outside the Tokyo area

● Holy Ghost Hospital (**Sei Rei Byoin**), Kawanayamacho Showa-ku, Nagoya 466. Tel: (052) 832-1181.

● Kobe Adventist Hospital, 4-1-8 Arinodai Kita-ku, Kobe 651. Tel: (078) 981-0161.

● Kobe Ekisaidai Hospital, 2-5-6 Nakayamate-dori Chuo-ku, Kobe 650. Tel: (078) 341-7291.

● Kobe Kaisei Hospital, 11-15-3 Shinohara Kita-machi, Nada-ku, Kobe 657. Tel: (078) 871-5201-5.

● Nagoya University Hospital, Maitsurucho Showa-ku, Nagoya 466. Tel (052) 741-2111.

● Osaka National Hospital, 1-14-2 Hoenzaka Chuo-ku, Osaka 540. Tel: (06) 942-1331.

● Osaka University Hospital, 4-3-57 Nakanoshima Kita-ku, Osaka 530. Tel: (06) 451-0051.

● The Japan Baptist Hospital, 47 Yamanomotocho Kita-Shirakawa, Sakyo-ku, Kyoto 606. Tel: (075) 781-5194.

DENTAL CARE

Dental care in Japan is of high quality but expensive. Japanese dentists do not usually take full-mouth x-rays but will tap and examine the teeth with instruments and/or take an x-ray of the tooth causing trouble. They are skilled at root canal and capping procedures. It would probably be better, and cheaper, to have needed dental and orthodontic work done before you go to Japan. Dental work in Japan is often done in stages and takes months to complete. Bills can be astronomical, so much so that some people actually fly to Taiwan or Hong Kong for dental care, because even with the air fare added in, there are significant savings. Braces are unusual. The Japanese do not place the same value on straight teeth as Westerners do; in fact, protruding incisors are considered cute.

The following dental offices and many others employ English-speaking staff.

● Japan-American Dental Clinic, 22-6-302 Saiwacho. Kanagawa-ken, Chigasaki-shi 253. Tel: (0467) 86-5502.

● Oyama Dental Office, New Otani Hotel, Kioicho 4-1 Chiyoda-ku, Tokyo. Tel: (03) 265-7587.

EMERGENCY SERVICES

The quickest way to get an ambulance in all cities is to dial 119; the operators, however, only speak Japanese. To ask for an ambulance, say 'kyu-kyusha onegai shimasu,' pronounced 'cue-sha-o-ne-guy-she-mus.' In addition, you will need to give your address in Japanese. If this seems to complicated, you can call English-speaking operators (see list below); unfortunately, not all of them speak English fluently. Speak slowly and clearly and give your full address.

In Tokyo:	(03)	212-2323
In Kobe:	(078)	391-6931
In Osaka:	(06)	531-0601
In Kyoto:	(075)	23-3511

If you are in the Tokyo area and have an emergency requiring assistance, there are 24-hour emergency numbers staffed by fluent English-speaking personnel:

Police:	(03)	581-4321
Japan Red Cross:	(03)	400-1211
Yokohama Fire Station:	(045)	33-46789

COUNSELLING SERVICES

The **Tokyo English Life Line** (TELL) is a church-sponsored service for foreigners offering anonymous, free telephone counselling for family, emotional, or social problems. The phones are answered by trained volunteer counsellors.

Tel: (03) 264-4347
Hours: 9.00 am to 4.00 pm and 7.00 pm to 11.00 pm daily

The **Tokyo Community Counselling Service** (TCCS) is a professionally staffed organisation with English-speaking specialists in such areas as marital and family counselling, cultural adjustment, learning disabilities, and alcohol and drug abuse.

Tel: (03) 780-0336

HEALTH INSURANCE

If you belong to a health insurance plan they will probably extend your policy to cover you in Japan, but do check before you leave. Alternatively, you may apply for coverage under the Japanese National Health Insurance Program (**Kokumin Kenko Hoken**), which pays about 75 percent of all medical expenses. The premiums are based on the preceding year's salary in Japan, so the first year the payments will be negligible no matter what your job is. To apply for this insurance, simply go to your **shiyajusho** (town hall) and fill up an application form. The process will taken only a few minutes.

PHARMACIES

Japanese medicines are excellent and are distributed by hospital pharmacies. If you feel you really need a specific product, there are two Tokyo pharmacies (not connected with hospitals) which carry many internationally-known brands.

- American Pharmacy, Hibiy Park Building, 1-8-1 Yurakucho Chiyoda-ku, Tokyo. Tel: (03) 271-4035.

- Medical Dispensary, 32 Mori Building, 3-4-30 Shiba Koen Minato-ku, Tokyo. Tel: (03) 434-5817.

How to Get a Job Abroad
Roger Jones BA(Hons) DipEd DPA

Second Edition

This great value-for-money paperback is essential reading for everyone planning to spend a period abroad. A key feature is the lengthy reference section of medium and long-term job opportunities and possibilities, arranged by region and country of the world, and by profession/occupation. There are many more than 130 pages of specific contacts and leads, giving literally hundreds of addresses and much hard-to-find information. There is a classified guide to overseas recruitment agencies, and even a multi-lingual guide to writing application letters. The first edition of this popular handbook was published in 1989, and has since sold many thousands of copies. The book has now been thoroughly revised and updated in a new second edition: it contains many new addresses and entries, and reflects recent political developments in Europe, the Gulf, and other parts of the world.

From Reviews

'A fine book for anyone considering even a temporary overseas job.' *The Evening Star*. 'A highly informative and well researched book . . . containing lots of hard information and a first class reference section . . . A superb buy.' *The Escape Committee Newsletter*. Roger Jones BA AKC DipTESL DipEd MInstAm DPA MBIM has himself worked abroad for many years in such varied locations as Austria, Cambodia, Thailand, Turkey and the Middle East. A specialist writer on expatriate and employment matters, he is also author of **How to Teach Abroad** in the same series.
£9.99pb, 288pp illus. I 85703 003 6. 2nd edition

How To Books Ltd, Plymbridge House, Estover Road, Plymouth PL6 7PZ, United Kingdom. Tel: (0752) 695745. Fax: (0752) 695699. Telex: 45635.

9
Schools

THE JAPANESE EDUCATION SYSTEM

The Japanese educational system has received a great deal of publicity in recent years. Literacy rates of 99 percent and exceptional achievement in maths and science are considered by many to be major contributors to Japan's economic success. These accomplishments are the result of a strong commitment to high quality education. In 1947 compulsory education was extended from six to nine years. Today 94 percent of students go on to either state or private three-year upper secondary or high schools, and over one third of those continue on to higher education.

Students' abilities are judged on their past merits, including the quality of their previous education. Successful navigation of the system depends heavily on attendance at the 'right schools'. Parents, hoping to give their offspring the chance to secure top places in prestigious universities, will enrol their children in very competitive kindergartens or even preschools.

An intensive approach
From kindergarten to secondary school, education is the single most important aspect of life for Japanese children. It is highly focused and very intense. School children are in school for about eight hours a day, five and a half days a week, 210 days a year. The school year runs from April to March with very brief breaks based on the national holidays.

Daily homework is set from the very first year, and most students receive outside tutoring or attend private after school **yobiko** or **juku** (crammers) to help them prepare for high school and college entrance examinations. Discipline is strict in both state and private school systems. Dress codes include rules regarding the length of hair and width of pants or length of skirts. Make-up and hair colouring are not allowed.

Universities

The Japanese university system was founded in 1869 with the establishment of the National University which later became Tokyo University. Initially a huge majority of the best jobs were filled by individuals educated at this institution. As other institutions of higher learning were established, the most influential jobs remained in the control of people from the older universities who invariably selected people from their alma maters as their successors. In this way an old boy network was cemented in place, a network still highly operative to this day. The selection system for Japan's most prestigious companies is monopolised by the network of graduates who have gained hiring power and the graduates of the schools which they are indefinitely obligated to. One is thus firmly set upon the path to prosperity when one gains entrance to one of these universities.

Students begin preparing for the all important entrance examinations in the earliest years. The exams are fiercely competitive. When students are ready to leave high school they choose which universities they might like to go to and then take those institutions' entrance exams. The exams are only held at the institution campuses and only once a year for each school. If the student misses the exam at his first choice school, or for any reason or does not pass, he or she must wait until the following year to take the exam again. Individuals who delay college until they get into the school of their choice are called **ronin**, or wanderers.

Exam time is called 'examination hell' because of the pressure it puts on the students who know that the results will in large part determine the paths their lives will take. Once accepted at a university there is a marked decline in academic diligence as students realise that they have crossed the last major hurdle to a prosperous future.

ENTERING THE JAPANESE SYSTEM

One option for Western expatriates is to send their children to Japanese schools. Considering the intense competitiveness of the Japanese schools, however, most children unable to speak Japanese would be lost. Early entrance at preschool or kindergarten level may be feasible, however, giving the child the opportunity to pick up linguistic skills at the outset. Even children with high Japanese language ability are likely to meet learning difficulties later on.

Being very group-oriented, the Japanese develop strong walls to protect the groups from external threat and keep potentially disruptive outsiders from gaining entrance to the inner circle. This is often shown in difficulties that develop when Japanese respond to outsiders trying to gain access to a group, or when foreigners express their individuality in a way that threatens the group. This problem is especially apparent in the relationships between Japanese and foreign children.

Bullying has become a significant problem in recent years. There are children who commit suicide every year because of pressures placed on them and punishments they receive for being seen as different or not giving way to group norms. There have even been cases of students retaliating with murder. Although such cases are extremely rare, they are indicative of the difficulties newcomers to Japanese classrooms may face.

INTERNATIONAL SCHOOLS

The importance placed on education in Japan is reflected in the high quality of Japan's international schools. Finding adequate schooling for your children should not be a problem, especially if you live in or near a large metropolitan area. Most cities have international schools running from nursery to sixth form or twelfth grade level, and welcome new families. You can telephone the principal's office to arrange a visit to discuss the school's programme and inspect the facilities.

International schools offering a US curriculum are usually accredited by the appropriate American accrediting body and the curriculum is compatible with stateside schools. Those students often return home with a stronger academic record than their counterparts back home and are notably more mature and cosmopolitan in outlook. They may, however, fall a little behind in English-language skills, which is understandable. Study of the Japanese language is generally required in the lower years and most students soon master enough to get by on the street.

Since school is usually the centre of a youngster's educational and social life, both academic and extracurricular aspects of schooling should be taken into account. Academic interests may be balanced with sports and other after-school activities. Friendships are made with Japanese and other international students and are especially fostered by travel programmes, ski weekends, and the like.

Occasionally flare-ups of antiforeign feelings arise between Japanese and international students, sometimes resulting in fistfights, but it is not really a major problem for parents or students. In the large cities, especially Tokyo, alcohol and drugs have become a teenage problem, just as in so many other countries. These problems tend to be more acute if the parents themselves are finding it difficult to adapt to life abroad.

PRESCHOOL CHILDREN

Young mothers with preschoolers may have more problems than the parents of older children — there is not a great deal for youngsters to do. Most preschools and day care facilities for toddlers are tailored to the Japanese, and for linguistic and cultural reasons are difficult for the newly arrived expat to break into. Half-day nursery facilities are available in some areas, and there will generally be zoos and playgrounds to visit, as well as clubs and social groups that enable women to get together with other young mothers. To get a feel for the system, mothers of preschoolers should try to meet up with parents of slightly older children. This is possible by becoming active in school activities even though children are not yet in attendance.

SCHOOL ADDRESSES

Here is a list of international schools in Japan's major cities. This information can be a jumping off point for your search.

Fukuoka

- **Fukuoka International School**, 1-28-4 Maidashi, Higashi-ku, Fukuoka. Tel: (092) 641-0326. Founded in 1972; coeducational; grades K-9 with high school correspondence courses; total capacity 65 students; US curriculum.

Hiroshima

- **Hiroshima International School**, 3-49-1 Kurakake, Asa Kita-ku, Hiroshima, Tel: (082) 843-4111. Founded in 1962; coeducational; grades K-9 with ESL and culture programmes for grades 3-adult; 150 students; US/UK curriculum. Suburban/rural setting in new area of the city.

Kobe

- **Canadian Academy** 3-1-2 Nagamindai, Nada-ku, Kobe, Tel: (078) 881-5211. Founded in 1913; coeducational; grades K-12; boarding and day students; total capacity is 650 students; US curriculum. Located on Rokko Island.

- **Marist Brothers International School**, 2-1-1 Chimori-cho, Suma-ku, Kobe, Tel: (078) 732-6268. Founded in 1951; coeducational; grades K-12; total capacity is about 360 students; US curriculum. Located fifteen minutes from downtown Kobe. Sponsored by the Catholic Church.

- **St Michaels International School**, 17-2-3 Nakayamate-dori, Chuo-ku, Kobe, Tel: (078) 231-8885. Founded in 1946; coeducational; primary school; 182 students; UK curriculum. Sponsored by the Anglican Church.

Kyoto

- **Kyoto International School**, 11-1 Ushinomiya-cho, Yoshida, Sakyo-ku, Kyoto 606, Tel: (075) 771-4022. Founded in 1960; coeducational; grades 1-8; 90 students; US/UK curriculum. Classes are small; facilities consist of one building with eight classrooms.

Nagoya

- **Nagoya International School**, 2628 Minamihara, Nakashidami, Moriyama-ku, Nagoya, Tel: (052) 736-2025. Founded in 1964; coeducational; nursery- grade 12; 301 students; US curriculum. Located in suburban area of Nagoya, in a unique round building built in 1964. Most teachers are American; students about 50 percent American, 50 percent from nine other countries. Almost all graduates go on to college.

Osaka

Osaka is served by the schools in Kobe, which is only 30 minutes away.

Tokyo

- **Japan International School**, 5-20 Kamiyama-cho, Shibuya-ku, Tokyo. Tel: (03) 3468-8476. Founded in 1980; coeducational; grades 1-9; 350 students. Bilingual, all children learn Japanese. Affiliated with Aoba International School.

- **Nishimachi International School**, 14-7, Moto Azabu, 2-chome, Minato-ku, Tokyo 106, Tel: (03) 3451-5520. Founded in 1949; coeducational; kindergarten to grade 9; 350 students; US curriculum;

entrance tests required. In the heart of Tokyo, a ten-minute walk from the subway. Four buildings and a good library.

● **St Mary's International School**, 6-19 Seta 1-chome, Setagaya-ku, Tokyo 158, Tel: (03) 3709-4311. Founded in 1952; for boys only; grades 1-12; 800 students; US curriculum; International Baccalaureate; uniforms required. Very strong sports program. Good transportation to the seven-acre campus; modern equipment. High academic record; Roman Catholic faculty.

● **Seisen International School**, 12-15 Yoga 1-chome, Seta gaya-ku, Tokyo 158, Tel: (03) 3704-2661. Founded in 1952; girls allowed; kindergarten-grade 12; uniforms required; about 500 girls of twenty-three nationalities. Roman Catholic instruction. Good facilities; about 94 percent of the graduates go on to college.

● **The American School in Japan**, 1-1-1 Nomizu, Chofu-shi, Tokyo 182, Tel: (422) 31-6351. Founded in 1902; coeducational; preschool to grade 12; between 800 and 1,000 children from some twenty-five nationalities; US curriculum. Twelve-acre site in western suburbs of Tokyo; there is a school bus service, and a train runs to within a five-minute walk. Academic standards are high.

● **Aoba International School**, 2-10-34 Aobadai, Meguro-ku, Tokyo, Tel: (03) 3461-1442. Founded in 1976; coeducational; preschool for children ages 3 to 5; range of nationalities, but taught in English. Located between Nakameguro Station and Ohashi; can also be reached by bus from Shibuya or Nakameguro. Very well equipped.

● **Christian Academy in Japan**, 2-14, 1-chome, Shinkawa-cho, Higashi Kurume-shi, Tokyo 203, Tel: (0424) 71-0022. Founded in 1950; coeducational; boarding or day; about 350 children in grades 1-12; US curriculum; bilingual (3rd and 4th levels learn Japanese). College prep and industrial arts. About 80 percent of the students are the children of missionaries coming from many nations.

● **International School of the Sacred Heart**, 3-1 Hiroo 4-chome, Shibuya-ku, Tokyo 150, Tel: (03) 3400-3951. Founded in 1908 by the Catholic church; girls only; grades K-12 (kindergarten is coed); the 700 students come from about forty-nine countries; international curriculum; the faculty is also international.

Yokohama

- **St Joseph International School**, 85 Yamate-cho, Naka-ku, Yokohama, Tel (045) 641-0065. Founded in 1901; coeducational; prekindergarten to grade 12; 450 students; US curriculum. Sponsored by Marianists of Japan.

- **Saint Maur International School**, 83 Yamate-cho, Naka-ku, Yokohama 231, Tel: (045) 641-5751. Founded in 1872; coeducational; about 360 students in grades 1-12; US curriculum; primarily college prep. New, well-equipped building includes home economics department, science labs, and library. Nursery school: 100 children, coeducational, ages 21/2 to 5; Montessori method.

- **Yokohama International School**, 258 Yamate-cho, Naka-ku, Yokohama 231, Tel: (045) 622-0084. Founded in 1924 for children of all nationalities; coeducational; prekindergarten to sixth-form/grade 13; 366 students; US/UK curriculum. Children come from twenty countries and 35 faculty of seven nationalities. Good facilities; classes are kept small; good college prep record.

Okinawa

- Okinawa Christian School, PO Box 42, 1300 Aza Makiminato, Urasoe, Okinawa 901-21, Tel: (0988) 773661. Founded in 1957; coeducational, private, nonprofit; prekindergarten to grade 12; 370 students; US curriculum.

Sapporo

- Hokkaido International School, 5-35-2 3-jo, Fukuzumi, Toyohira-ku, Sapporo, Tel: (011) 851-1205. Founded in 1958; coeducational; Grades 1-12, private nonprofit. US curriculum. Located about ten miles from central Sapporo.

INTERNATIONAL COLLEGES AND UNIVERSITIES

Tokyo

- International Division, Jochi (Sophia) University, 7-1 Kioicho, Chiyoda-ku, Tokyo 102, Tel: (03) 3238-4018. Founded in 1949; this is a Jesuit university with roughly 1,000 students each term/semester and a faculty of 60. Terms start in September, December, and March; there is also a summer session and an evening school. Internationally accredited courses lead to a bachelor's degree, if desired. Twelve credit hours may be taken each semester and six credit hours in summer.

- **International Christian University**, 10-2, Osawa, 3-chome, Mitaka-shi, Tokyo 181, Tel: (0422) 33-3131. Founded in 1949, ICU is a four-year liberal arts university with a wide range of majors. Its 1,730 undergraduates and 159 graduate students, 154 of which are non-Japanese, come from twenty nations. Japanese students start in the spring term, all others in the autumn. There is a 220-acre campus, with an excellent library, eight dormitories, several gyms and pools.

EDUCATIONAL INFORMATION

For general information contact:

Japan-US Educational Commision
Rm. 207 Sanno Grand Building
2-14-2 Nagatacho, Chiyoda-ku, Tokyo.
Tel: (03) 580-3231.
Open 9.00 am to 5.00 pm. Closed Saturday and Sunday.

10
Cars and Driving

CONGESTION AND DELAYS

Driving in Japan has its benefits, but the hazards, high costs, and prodigious amounts of red tape involved for natives and foreigners alike can be discouraging. Many people avoid cars and driving entirely.

Traffic moves on the left side of the road as in Britain. Roads are very crowded and generally very narrow, sometimes without pavements, and blind alleys are common. Cars must share the limited street space with a multitude of delivery trucks, motorcycles, bicycles and pedestrians. Afternoon and evening traffic is especially heavy, so it is best to drive early in the day if possible. Signs are in Japanese in most areas, but on major highways they are generally international. Driving in Japan can definitely be a challenging experience.

Tolls and speedlimits
Tolls on most highways are steep, from about £4 to £20. The speed limit on highways is 80 kph (50 mph) and on most city streets 30-40 kph. You will not usually have to worry about exceeding the speed limit while driving in the big cities, however, since most of the day metropolitan traffic moves no faster than a crawl.

BUYING AND MAINTAINING A CAR

Many people buy secondhand European and American cars, but Japanese cars are less expensive and are better geared to the narrow, twisting streets. The cost of maintenance, road taxes, and other expenses are lower as well. Since Japan imports all of its petroleum, the price of fuel is quite high; all the more reason to buy a small car. The Japanese are well known for their good service, so repairs should be no problem (except for the expense).

Inspections

One of the main headaches for a car owner in Japan is the compulsory inspection which is required at least every two years; it is also required when you register the car, when you renew registration, and when the car changes ownership. Only special garages can do the inspection, and you must plough through reams of paperwork in the process. Most foreigners end up paying a substantial fee to have someone do the inspection for them. Ask your friends and colleagues about all the miseries of this procedure before you acquire a car.

Car insurance

Car insurance is compulsory. At least two American insurance companies have branch offices throughout Japan: American International Underwriters and the Great American Insurance Company. The British Insurance Group also provides good coverage. Adequate liability coverage is especially important because the car driver is, by custom, nearly always liable to the injured person, and enormous amounts of money can be involved.

● For general car and driving information, consult the **Japan Automobile Federation**, 5-8 Shiba Park 3-chome, Minato-ku, Tokyo. Tel: (03) 436-2811.

DRIVING LICENCES

An international driver's licence is valid in Japan for only one year and is not renewable. A foreign licence, however, is not valid. If you plan to do a lot of driving, you should obtain a Japanese licence.

If you have a valid driving licence from your home country, getting a Japanese licence is relatively painless. It is obtained at the licence office nearest your place of residence. Your ward office will give you the address. You should bring your current driver's licence, your passport, and your alien registration card. Total fees are between Y3000 and Y4000. A normal passenger car licence also covers 50cc motor scooters, which are a convenient option for commuting. You will be asked to take an eye examination, which consists of reading the usual charts, and a colour-blindness test.

Your Japanese driving licence will be valid until your third birthday after the date of issue. If you stay in Japan that long, be sure to renew your licence within one month before it expires. Only an eye examination will be required for the renewal. If your licence expires, the red tape involved in obtaining a new one is considerable.

Without a foreign or international driving licence, you will be tested not only on your driving ability but on your knowledge about the engine and the mechanics of the car and on your ability to repair it as well. This is the test that Japanese must pass, and many of them have to take the examination several times before they obtain a licence. To prepare for this stringent examination, the Japanese attend a rather lengthy and expensive driving school. Deciding to drive in Japan without a foreign licence is starting the hard way.

11
Japan at Leisure

Leisure is very important to the Japanese. The pace of life is hectic, and the style in which they manage their personal and business affairs creates a great deal of tension. The Japanese need relaxation, and they plan it carefully. So too should the visitor living in Japan. It is easy to fall into a nonstop work routine which can be detrimental to your health, let alone your sanity. There are so many activities to choose from and so many ways to be entertained that it should not be hard to find and maintain a healthy balance between work and play.

EATING AND DRINKING

There is an unbelievable variety of food and eating establishments from which to choose in Japan. The Japanese place a great deal of emphasis on the environment in which they eat — anywhere from the jolly conviviality of the neighbourhood noodle shop to the calm of a temple cloister. There are restaurants set in the serenity of gardens with lotus ponds and ancient pines as well as fast-food franchises like McDonalds and Kentucky Fried Chicken. Many restaurants serve foreign cuisines; those from other Asian countries and from India are very popular.

Traditional foods
The Japanese, like the French, pay special attention to the manner in which meals are presented. The setting and service at a good Japanese restaurant can be a delightful aesthetic experience, to the eye as well as to the palate. Food is often served separately in small dishes to allow the unique flavours of each item to be savoured. Pay particular attention to the harmony of shapes, colours, and decorations, and to the contrast in textures as you sample the various elements of your meal.

Japanese cuisine provides a rich, varied, and satisfying range of culinary experiences. The foundation of the Japanese diet is, of course, rice. This is usually eaten boiled with various side dishes including combinations of salty vegetables, seafood, or soup.

Fish and other seafood are served in every possible way — raw, dried, broiled, boiled, pickled, salted, and fried. The entire fish, including the head, is often served, whether broiled or dried. The Japanese counterpart to the Western sandwich is **onigiri**, rice balls wrapped in dried seaweed, or **o-bento**, cold rice in a wooden or lacquer box, with perhaps broiled eel, vegetables, or pickles. Onigiri and o-bento are also often served at Kabuki or other theatrical performances and are available in railway stations. They make a pleasant meal on a train.

Some popular dishes

The more common Japanese dishes served for dinner or special events are listed below.

● **Sukiyaki** is the Japanese dish most popular and well known to foreigners. It is prepared by simmering thinly sliced beef together with various vegetables such as sliced onions, bean curd, and mushrooms in soy sauce and sake.

● **Tempura** is prepared by dipping prawns, fish, and vegetables in a light batter and deep-frying them in oil. Tempura is eaten hot with a sauce of **mirin** (sweet rice wine), soy sauce, and grated white radish and ginger.

● **Nimono** are boiled dishes consisting mainly of vegetables. These are cooked in stock made from **katsuo-bushi** (dried bonito flakes) and seasoned with sake, **mirin** (sweet rice wine), and other foods that add to the flavour. These dishes are common fare throughout Japan.

● **Mizutaki** is cooked in an earthenware pot and consists of chicken, various kinds of vegetables, and soup stock made from seaweed and dried bonito. It is dipped in a special sauce made from Japanese sake, soy sauce, citrus fruit juice, white radish, and sliced onion.

● **Kabayaki**, or broiled eel, is a delicacy favoured by the Japanese people for its high nutritional value as well as its mouth-watering taste. The prepared eel, cut to suitable lengths, is skewered, steamed to remove excess oil, and then placed over an open charcoal fire. It is dipped repeatedly into a special soy sauce (**tare**) during the broiling process. Eel is expensive and is usually eaten during hot weather, when it is in season.

● **Kaiseki** cuisine is considered to be the tops in Japanese cookery. It was originally served to guests before a tea ceremony and is distinguished by the use of vegetables for its seasoning base. Fish is the main ingredient, and great attention is paid to making it tasty and enjoyable. Various sizes, shapes, and colours of plates and bowls are chosen with the greatest care to complement the hues and forms of the foods served.

● **Sushi**, a popular Japanese food, is made by placing various kinds of vegetables and seafood, raw and prepared, on cold vinegared rice patties. Contrary to generally held Western beliefs, sushi refers to the use of cold flavoured rice and does not necessarily entail the use of raw fish. Cucumber, pickled radish, and sweet egg omelette are common components. It is usually eaten dipped in a little soy sauce and spiced up by a touch of **Wasabi**, very hot green horseradish. A bit or two of highly spiced, pickled ginger is eaten between varieties to clean the palate and prepare the mouth for the next taste.

● **Jingishu Kan Barbecue** is composed of thin slices of choice mutton grilled with such things as onion, cabbage, bean sprouts, and mushrooms, and is dipped in seasoned soy sauce before it is eaten.

Another Japanese favourite is noodle soup, which many foreigners come to love as well. There are several varieties of noodle used and many variations on the basic recipes. **Ramen** (thin noodles) and **udon** (thick noodles) will be the most common types that you encounter. A bowl of **ramen** at one of the abundant noodle shops can cost as little as Y200. For a little extra the chef will add a deep-fried shrimp or other delicacy to your dish. Preparation of good noodle soup demands real culinary skill.

Alcoholic drinks
Japan is famous for its rice wine **sake** (pronounced sah-kay), served warm in tiny cups. Partners at a meal go through a pleasant and gracious ritual of filling each other's cups, which serves to reinforce the personal relationships so vital to social interaction. Many Japanese men drink their sake cold (unheated), but unheated sake contains low levels of methyl alcohol, so beware.

Much to many foreigners' surprise, sake is not the most popular alcoholic drink in Japan. Beer consumption far surpasses that of sake and all other alcoholic beverages combined. Four major beer companies (Kirin, Suntory, Sapporo and Asahi) compete for the market, all with their separate brands of draught beer, lager, and malt. They have also recently begun producing new types of beer to expand their market share — dry, cool, winter, 5.5 percent, and Super Yeast beers. The Japanese also make very good whisky, with Suntory being the most popular.

Breakfast
Japanese-style breakfasts are not complete without boiled rice, raw eggs, fermented soybeans, pickles or **tsukemono** (tea) and **miso shiru**, a soup made with soy bean paste, vegetables and/or bean curd. Modern 'Tokyoites', however, and many young people, may prefer Western-style breakfasts of eggs, toast, and tea or coffee.

Street foods
An impressive array of foods is also available from street stalls and at festivals. Some of the most common are the following.

- **Oden**. Pieces of hot fish and vegetables cakes, hard boiled eggs, seaweed, and tofu boiled in broth. Pieces are served on bamboo skewers, and hot mustard spices ad to the flavour. The price is by the piece or by the plate.

- **Tako Yaki**. A small dumpling (eaten with a toothpick) made from wheat batter, onion, ginger, and chopped octopus. It is vaguely reminiscent of a clam fritter from the Deep South in the United States. A spicy sauce and a sprinkle of dry seaweed reminds you that you are in Japan.

- **Okonomiyaki**. Often called a Japanese pancake, this version is a very distant cousin of its Western counterpart. Okonomiyaki is made mostly of cabbage and egg with a little flour thrown in to hold it all together. The 'pancakes' are fried on a hot griddle and embellished with a variety of ingredients including various types of vegetables and fish.

- **Tomorokoshi**. Chicken (or liver) skewered on bamboo and broiled over charcoal. The sauce is especially delicious, made of soy sauce, rice wine vinegar, and sugar. This is also served as an hors d'oeuvre.

- **Okashi**. Traditional, sugar-coated sweets made of popped rice and other ingredients in various shapes and colours.

- **Ika Yaki**. A whole squid charcoal-grilled on a skewer. Don't be squeamish; it's delicious, although it is a relatively expensive treat.

Some Westerners are reluctant to try the unaccustomed flavours, textures, and combinations of Japanese food. Try to put aside any food prejudices you may have and explore these new tastes. The Japanese enjoy introducing guests to their favourite dishes, so your ability to appreciate Japanese food will contribute to good relationships with your Japanese acquaintances.

THE ARTS

Many of the arts in Japan reflect the characteristic Japanese perception of beauty, which emphasises simplicity and naturalness. In Japanese paintings nature is the predominant subject, and simple brush strokes, frequently on pure white backgrounds, are used to create vivid images. Japanese aesthetic taste is particularly striking in the famous landscape gardens. Created by Zen masters, these gardens are often characterised by the dominance of uncluttered space broken only by a few carefully placed objects. Nothing could better exemplify the tranquillity, subjectivity, and carefully cultivated harmony so central to Japanese values.

The following are among the most important of the traditional arts in Japan.

Haiku
A stylised and elegant form of poetry, haiku is a poem made up of seventeen syllables arranged in three lines of five, seven, and five syllables each. Traditional haiku themes are nature and life.

Ikebana
Ikebana is the art of flower arrangement, emphasising the recreation of the natural forms. Flowers,leaves, and branches are arranged in three levels so as to represent the sky, humanity, and earth in the harmonious balance of nature.

Bonsai
Bonsai, the art of cultivating dwarf trees, is perhaps the art form most familiar to Westerners. Bonsai are created by planting a tree and controlling

its growth and shape through transplanting, trimming, and other techniques. Bonsai can be seen in gardens throughout Japan.

Origami
The many decorative and ornamental designs of origami are made by folding paper according to specific guidelines. Origami is taught mostly to children, but almost everyone in Japan can make something if handed a piece of origami paper.

Cha-no yu
The Japanese tea ceremony, cha-no-yu, consists of the ritual making and serving of tea to honoured guests. It is frequently performed in a small building, detached from the home and specially designed for that purpose. Its aim is to foster gracefulness, inner harmony, and an appreciation of beauty in the natural simplicity of the ceremony.

MUSIC, THEATRE, AND FILMS

The Japanese enjoy music, both traditional and Western, so there is a rich variety of concerts for foreign visitors to choose from. Traditional Japanese music includes **shakuhachi** (Japanese flute) and **koto**, a Japanese stringed instrument. Western musical offerings range from symphony orchestras to jazz and rock. The price of tickets to any musical event, unfortunately, is very high. Visitors to Japan will want to sample the major traditional forms of Japanese theatre. Although the shows last five or six hours, you are free to attend for only a portion of that time. Outstanding puppet shows, revues, and light opera are also popular.

Kabuki
Kabuki theatre is similar in general themes to Western drama and could be called a sort of Japanese soap opera. Dialogue is accompanied by music and male actors play both male and female roles. The actors wear elaborate costumes and makeup, and the stories are complex and dramatic. Kabuki is performed regularly in the famous playhouses of all major cities in Japan, including the most famous, the **Kabukiza**, in Tokyo.

Noh
Still widely performed today, Noh is the oldest form of Japanese theatre. It is a highly stylised dance drama in which the actors wear costumes and masks of ancient tradition. In the days of the Shogun, Noh, which deals

with historical subjects and Buddhist themes, was performed for the aristocracy; Kabuki, for the people.

Takarazuka

Takarazuka is Japanese opera, consisting only of female performers, who play both male and female roles. The shows are musical renditions of both Japanese and Western stories. Takarazuka is quite popular with older Japanese.

Modern plays and films

Modern Western plays (in Japanese translation) also abound. At any one time, these may range from Shakespeare and Chekhov to Beckett and Pinter. In addition, the Theatre Club at Camp Zama (a US military base) presents plays in English from time to time. Finally, there are lots of cinemas showing foreign films. These are generally in the original language with Japanese subtitles. Cinema prices are high — about £7 to £10. A full list of current films is printed in all the English-language newspapers.

LIVING NATIONAL TREASURES

The Japanese have a system for honouring and rewarding artists who achieve mastery of their crafts. Individuals who are uniquely skilled in a particular Japanese art or craft such as kabuki, noh, pottery making, or metalwork are designated 'important cultural properties' and are known as Living National Treasures. A great deal of honour and prestige accompanies this designation. The artists are given annual grants so that they can train others and perpetuate their art, thus ensuring that the arts and crafts will not die out. Individuals do not receive a great deal of personal publicity but they are well known to others who practise the craft or follow it closely.

DIVERSIONS

You might want to sample some of Japan's most popular board games and informal leisure activities early on, both to see how much you enjoy them and to learn about another side of Japanese culture.

Go

A strategic game using black and white stones on a square board, go requires two players. The object is to enclose the largest area of space with your stones.

Shogi
Shogi is Chinese-style chess. The object is for the two players to immobilise each other's king and capture him. Both Go and shogi are considered intellectual games and are played professionally.

Mah-jongg
Mah-jongg, a game usually played for fun or for money, was introduced to Japan in the 1920s from China. It has become very popular; there are Mah-jongg parlours all over Japan.

Manga
There are manga (Japanese comic books) on every conceivable subject: sports, hobbies, special interests, history, cooking, survival, sex and sadism, and on and on. Almost everyone reads them — housewives and salarymen (white-collar office workers and midlevel supervisors and executives) as well as young people. Most are drawn by skilled artists.

Pachinko
Pachinko is a pinball game that uses small steel balls in a vertical slot machine. Many people sell their prizes back to the parlours for money, thus making it a gambling game (which is illegal but winked at by the authorities). The name comes from the sound the balls make when shot into the machine. Gaudy pachinko parlours can be found virtually anywhere in Japan.

SPORTS

The three sports most widely followed in Japan are golf (the Saturday company golf games are an accepted part of the work week); baseball, mostly a spectator sport, and **sumo**, traditional Japanese wrestling, now popular on British television.

Other popular sports are judo, volleyball, skiing and karate. Gymnastics, soccer, swimming, diving, horse racing, car racing, tennis, badminton, squash, basketball, bowling, and skating are also pursued to some extent. Tennis is popular among the expatriate set.

Sports clubs and facilities
Many of the best sports facilities are found in private clubs, where membership is costly. It has been reported that 'Tennis clubs, golf courses, etc, are beyond the easy reach of most individuals and indeed of many companies. Fees are horrendous.' Many corporations maintain club

memberships for their expatriate managers, so enquire about company arrangements first. Resort hotels also offer access to sports facilities to their guests, and expatriates have been known to check in for a weekend to take advantage of such offers.

To find out more about sports clubs and facilities, ask at the big hotels, scan the English-language newspapers for club events and activities, or contact the Japan National Tourist Organization (JNTO).

Golf

Japan is understandably proud of its golf courses. There are some outstanding ones in several resort areas: the Kawana Hotel (two eighteen-hole courses) in Ito (Shizuoka Prefecture); Hakonen Golf Course, Dai-Hakone Country Club, and Hakone Kurakake Golf Course in Kanagawa Prefecture; and the Fuji Golf Course in Yamanashi Prefecture Remember, however, that private clubs are staggeringly expensive and that public courses are crowded and costly as well. The best idea for golf enthusiasts is to write the Japan Golf Association (see Appendix) for information about guest arrangements and possible memberships.

Baseball

Baseball was introduced into Japan in 1873 and has a long history in the Islands of the Rising Sun. There are two professional leagues, each with six corporate-sponsored teams, and the season culminates with a World Series. The Yomiuri Giants in Tokyo are the New York Yankees of Japan.

The semiannual all-Japan high school baseball tournament at Koshien Stadium in Osaka is probably the single most popular sports event in the country. Tokyo's Big Six University League (one of several) featuring such traditional powerhouses as Waseda and Keio, also generates widespread enthusiasm. For younger children, there is even Little League.

For an introduction to the sport of baseball as it reflects Japanese attitudes and culture, see Robert Whiting's *The Chrysanthemum and the Bat* on sale at most bookstores that handle foreign-language publications.

Sumo

No overview of sports in Japan would be complete without some mention of **sumo**, the ancient ritualised form of wrestling that even the most sceptical of foreign observers will concede ranks among the world's most fascinating sports.

The pride that the Japanese take in this traditional form of encounter goes beyond their fondness for baseball, golf, bowling, or any other imported sport. It is, like the wood-block print, kabuki, and haiku, a creation unique to Japan, and as such highly valued.

American interest in the sport was enhanced some years ago by the emergence of a Hawaiian (ring name: Takamiyama) as one of the more successful and popular wrestlers. His book, *Takamiyama*, coauthored by long-time sumophile, John Wheeler, provides a wrestler's-eye view not simply of the sport itself, but of the tradition that surrounds it. Recently another Hawaiian (ring name: Konishiki) has risen to one of the highest ranks in sumo and has a large following.

There are sumo tournaments six times a year in Japan, every other month. Each tournament lasts for fifteen days, and each one is broadcast for two or more hours a day on NHK, the public television channel. Try to cultivate a taste for sumo. Like learning the language and eating the food, being able to appreciate sumo will enhance your standing among neighbours, office colleagues, and business associates, and deepen your understanding of Japanese culture.

Skiing

This is a popular sport in Japan and there are many good resorts with a great variety of practice hills, lifts, tows, and jumping facilities. A number of resorts boast lovely hotels and inns, many of them with hot-spring baths to slip into after a hard day on the slopes. The primary ski area is located in the 'Japanese alps' in the Nagano area of central Japan. There is also excellent skiing in Hokkaido from early autumn to late spring. Most areas are packed at weekends and on holidays, so midweek skiing is preferable.

You can rent equipment almost everywhere, although you may have trouble if your feet are big or if you are very tall. Costs range from £20 to £40 for an all-day ski pass. The best way to get to the slopes is by the many special ski trains. If you can get a second-class reserved seat in advance, you will pay about half what it costs in first class.

Judo

Judo is indigenous to Japan; its roots can be traced back to early times. It is a kind of wrestling in which one uses flowing movements to exploit the momentum of one's opponents in throwing them down. You can watch experts any time at the famous Kodokan in Tokyo.

Karate

Karate originated in China and came to Japan via Okinawa, but it too has now been completely 'Japanised' and taken up by thousands in Japan as well as throughout the world. You can take lessons or watch classes at the headquarters of the Japan Karate Association, near Ebisu station in Tokyo.

Tennis

For those who play tennis and can afford the fees, the Tokyo Lawn Tennis club has excellent facilities. Your time on the waiting list can be shortened by sending off your application before you arrive: 1-8 Azabu Morioka-cho, Minato-ku, Tokyo. In the Osaka-Kobe region the Kobe Regatta and Athletic Club (KRAC) and the Shioya Country club (thirty minutes west of Kobe) offer tennis, swimming, and other sports. There are also a number of social clubs in the area with sports facilities.

FESTIVALS

In the course of a year, nearly every city, village, temple, and shrine sponsors a festival, known as a **matsuri**. Music, the roll of drums, processions of people, and brightly coloured decorations are everywhere. In large cities such as Tokyo and Osaka, festivals seem to be celebrated continuously. Each is special to one group of people whose celebration is joined by thousands of well-wishers, visitors, and tourists.

Festivals originated in the early days of Japan when people communicated joyously with their gods, hoping to win favour and bring blessings on their neighbourhoods or their work. Religious sentiments still form the core of many festivals, though few Japanese are active members of religious organisations.

The presence of the gods is symbolised by the carrying of a gaudily decorated **omikoshi**, a small portable shrine borne on the shoulders of the male members of the local association. The carefree spirit with which this is done is impressive; exuberance and joy are the hallmarks of these occasions. Joining the festive crowds as often as possible is a good way not only to learn your city but also to see Japanese families totally relaxed and enjoying themselves.

Each issue of the *Tour Companion* (a free weekly newspaper available at all major hotels) gives the history and details of one major matsuri. Maps with subway information are included.

TRAVEL IN JAPAN

Travel in Japan is exceptionally pleasant, rewarding, and really quite easy, but it does take a little motivation, a good guidebook, some Japanese phrases, and a lot of money. Those who limit themselves to Tokyo or other big cities miss a great deal. Outside the cities Japan is a delight for the visiting foreigner. This is true partly because the Japanese feel responsible for their visitors' welfare and partly because travel facilities are better developed than anywhere else in Asia. It is true also because Japan is simply a beautiful country, with settings to satisfy all tastes. You can choose warm seascapes or rugged snow-covered mountains any time of the year. Between the mountain ranges are fertile valleys dotted with lakes; streams and rivers cut deep gorges and ravines in the mountains, cascading down in brilliant waterfalls. Because the coastline is so irregular, it is almost twice as long as that of the United States, providing magnificent vistas of rugged mountains jutting up from the sea as well as a wealth of harbours.

- The **Japan Grey Line**, a sight-seeing company, runs bus tours in English all over Japan. They run half-day and full-day tours of Tokyo, evening tours of Kabuki shows and Geisha parties, one- or two-day trips to Mt Fuji, and many other excursions. Someone is available to accept reservations in English 24 hours a day (see Appendix for address).

Not to miss

Kamakura
Just outside Tokyo lies Kamakura, an ancient city and home of the famous outdoor Giant Buddha and many notable temples. From Tokyo you can easily get to the lofty Alps in central Honshu. From the highest mountain peaks you can see both the Pacific Ocean and the Japan Sea. More than 250 volcanic peaks rise higher than 6,000 feet, some to 9,000, and Mt Fuji to more than 12,000. Nearly 200 of the volcanoes are still active. In the summer months it is possible to climb Mt Fuji (don't be surprised to find little old ladies passing you on the way up).

Nikko
To the north of Tokyo, Nikko is another easy trip. It is a beautiful mountainous area with many ancient temples. Nikko is also the site of a winter carnival which includes the creation of an enormous ice city including long slides and an impressive two-storey ice castle.

Kyoto
Once the capital and centre of Japanese culture, Kyoto has hundreds of temples and other sacred edifices, including Kiyomizu, the huge temple complex located on the eastern mountain overlooking the city; the Silver

and Golden Pavilions (Ginkaku-ji and Kinkaku-ji); and the stunning rock garden of Ryoan-ji.

Nara
South of Kyoto lies Nara. Older than Kyoto, Nara was the first capital of Japan and is home to the largest wooden structure in the world, which houses another Giant Buddha. Nara is a popular destination for Japanese and non-Japanese tourists alike. Many of the city's points of interest are located within easy walking distance of each other, which makes the area ideal for day trips.

Boso/Kyushu
The tea plantations of Shizuoka and the coast of the Boso Peninsula are other favourite destinations. The southern island of Kyushu is a warm and beautiful area all year round. As you go to these or other areas, whether by train, bus, or car, you will be able to see a lot of the rural lifestyle and farming methods. Only 16 percent of the mountainous islands can be farmed. Even when you pass through densely populated areas, you may still see terraced rice fields climbing up the sides of mountains.

Hokkaido
The Izu Peninsula, west of Tokyo, is a beautiful area in the summer. In the winter try to get to Sapporo on the northern island of Hokkaido. Their winter festival is one of the best, with giant snow sculptures dwarfing the surrounding office buildings. Hokkaido is less populated than the other large islands of Japan and architecturally the most Europeanised. The chilly climate of Hokkaido provides excellent skiing and is in stark contrast to the warmer areas of the southern islands.

Ryokans (inns)
In major cities and tourist areas throughout Japan you will find Western-style hotels, but there are also many **ryokans**, the famous Japanese inns. There are over 80,000 ryokans in Japan. They provide a pleasant and memorable experience which can bring one closer to the Japanese than their Euro-American equivalents.

Travel planning
You may want to work out travel plans before you leave home. If so, contact Japan Air Lines, Japan National Tourist Organization, or the Japan Travel Bureau. Keep in mind, however, that you may be able to make better arrangements once you arrive in Japan. Trains and buses are, as

previously discussed, punctual, clean, generally inexpensive, but often crowded.

● You may wish to obtain a **Japan Rail Pass**, which allows the bearer unlimited travel on all Japan Railway trains, including the Shinkansen, the bullet train, for a specified period of time. It must be purchased outside Japan and used within one year of the purchase date. For Rail Pass information, contact any international tourist agency.

For further tourist or travel information, you can explore the many travel guides about Japan or the numerous English language newspapers and journals which will provide current information on happenings of interest. In the Tokyo area, the *Tokyo Journal* or the *Tokyo Weekender* will provide information on all events in eastern Japan. Elsewhere, look for the *Discover Kinki* newspaper, which has all the information for the Osaka, Kyoto, and Kobe areas. All these publications are available in hotel lobbies or most bookshops.

12
The Major Cities

TOKYO

Overview

Tokyo is enormously exciting. Most visitors find it a dynamic city and enjoy being there despite the pressures and the costs. It is the centre of Japanese government, industry, finance, and culture. Culture in Tokyo is outstanding, far ahead of most other cities in Japan. Theatre of every variety flourishes; symphony orchestras compare well with those in Europe; the Japanese writers clustered in Tokyo produce some of the world's best current literature; and the city is the centre of outstanding contemporary architecture and industrial design.

Tokyo bridges two worlds — one is quite traditional, the other thoroughly twentieth century and on the move. Hundreds of modern buildings, including a number of skyscrapers, are changing the Tokyo skyline. There is a huge new metropolitan development of more than a dozen skyscrapers covering some 240 acres and eleven blocks. The Keio Plaza Hotel was the first of the tall buildings, forty-seven stories high. In the past, there was great reluctance to build upwards because fear of another major earthquake. Recent advances in architectural design, however, are believed to have overcome the dangers involved, and tall buildings are now common in Tokyo.

Some of the more affluent foreigners live in Western-style apartments or houses paying five or six times the rent they would pay outside Japan. Many foreigners, however, choose to live in more Japanese-style housing, which is more reasonable.

Already, millions of yen have been spent to build highways, design and develop a central park area, and build a massive rail and subway station for the more than 3.5 million people who live, work, shop, and play in the Shinjuku (western) section of Tokyo, now considered to be the heart of the city.

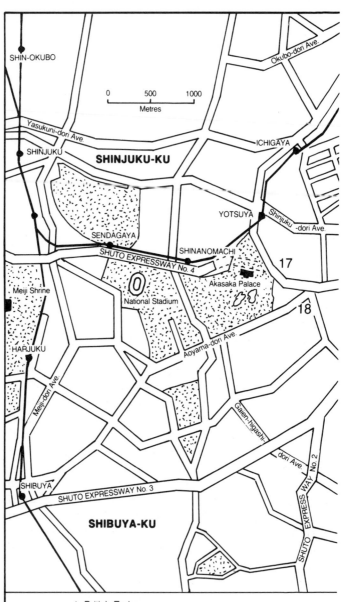

1. British Embassy
2. British Council
3. USA Embassy
4. World Trade Center Building
5. International Trade Centre
6. Tokyo Chamber of Commerce and Industry
7. Ministry of International Trade and Industry
8. Ministry of Foreign Affairs
9. Ministry of Finance
10. Japan Taxfree Center
11. St Lukes International Hospital

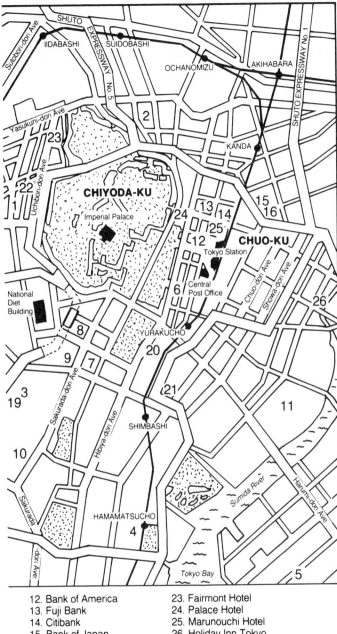

12. Bank of America
13. Fuji Bank
14. Citibank
15. Bank of Japan
16. Bank of Tokyo
17. Hotel New Otani
18. Akasaka Tokyu Hotel
19. ANA Hotel Tokyo
20. Imperial Hotel
21. Ginza Nikko Hotel
22. Diamond Hotel

23. Fairmont Hotel
24. Palace Hotel
25. Marunouchi Hotel
26. Holiday Inn Tokyo

One of the largest cities in the world, Tokyo is extremely densely populated, with over thirty million residents in the metropolitan area and surrounding conurbations. The city is a hodgepodge of factories, private homes, meat markets, night clubs, vegetable and fish shops, fancy hotels, and office skyscrapers. Land is at such a premium that the entire city has only six square miles of parks. The resulting urban problems are staggering.

Main problems for Tokyo-dwellers

Air pollution
Tokyo's factories discharge nearly two million tons of waste gases each year, and motor vehicles add an additional two million tons.

Traffic congestion
There is parking for only 90,000 of the two million cars in Tokyo, and cars average only twelve miles per hour through the clogged streets (about the speed of a bicycle). Buses are even slower.

Housing shortages
A million families are said to be living in substandard housing; about one-third of all buildings are wooden firetraps.

Water pollution
The Sumida River, which flows through Tokyo, is certainly no cleaner than the canals of Venice. Drains in most houses are open, and unpleasant smells are common.

With all these urban woes, and as disorganised and confusing as it can be, Tokyo has become a magnet of international finance and commerce and draws thousands of visitors each year.

Tokyo orientation

In the centre of Tokyo lies the Imperial Palace, where the emperor resides. The imperial grounds, which are open to tourists, contain beautiful gardens and are surrounded by moats. This is the location of the famous Budokan Hall, where major concerts and martial arts championship tournaments are held.

Just to the east of the imperial grounds are the Otemachi and Marunouchi areas — the centre of Tokyo's business district. Tokyo Station is located here. South of the imperial grounds lies the political centre of Tokyo, Nagatacho and Kasumigaseki. Here the Diet building and all ministries are located. A little to the east of the political centre and south of Marunouchi lies the well-known Ginza shopping area. To the west of the Imperial Palace is the beautiful Meiji Shrine and the major areas of Shibuya and Shinjuku. To the north is Ueno, where the famous Tokyo zoo is located, and Ikebukuro, a big shopping area. Ikebukuro station is one of the most confusing because the Eastern Store is located at the western exit and the Western Store is located at the eastern exit. Be sure to carry a map with you on your first few times out.

The main shopping areas in Tokyo are in Shinjuku, Shibuya, Ikebukuro, and — classiest of all — the Ginza. Two trendy shopping areas frequented by the young are Roppongo and Harajuku. The latest in fashions and other things Western or inspired by Western styles can be found there, especially in Harajuku.

For a taste of Japanese shopping less influenced by the West, try an area which the Japanese refer to as **shitamachi** ('downtown') called **Asakusa** (pronounced ah-sox-ah). Also, most neighbourhoods in and around Tokyo are a fascinating mix of traditional shops, boutiques, and department stores.

As in any city, there are areas which specialise in particular products. The Akihabara area specialises in shops selling only electrical appliances. In Jimbocho nearly a hundred little bookstores selling new and used books line the streets.

Transport in Tokyo

Taxis are usually plentiful but can be scarce during rush hours. There are taxi stands at all hotels and train stations, or you can hail them in the street.

Tokyo's extensive rail network provides services to every part of the city. Ten different subway lines criss-cross back and forth through the centre of Tokyo. The most important train line is the **Yamanote line**, which runs in a loop around central Tokyo. Major stops include Tokyo, Ueno, Ikebukuro, Shinjuku, and Shibuya. Most of the other trains run from the loop to the outlying areas. Trains and subways run every three to five minutes from about 4.30 am to 1.00 am.

Tokyo also has many buses. As said before, the signs are in Japanese, but once you know your route, buses are very convenient.

Finding addresses in Tokyo has been known to cause many headaches. Most businesses and stores can be located by identifying the nearest train or subway station. If you are having trouble finding an address, stop at one of the many police boxes, and ask the policeman for directions. If you know the name of your destination or have it written in Japanese, they will help you as best as they can, even if they don't speak English.

Tourist information services

Japan Travel-phone is a country-wide service offering information in English. The telephone number for the Tokyo area is 03-35021461; hours are 9.00 am to 5.00 pm daily.

Tours, temple celebrations, festivals, and other events occur constantly in Tokyo. Contact the Japan National Tourist Organisation for details. Besides the more common tourist attractions, Tokyo offers some additional, and quite interesting, opportunities to the visitor. Japan's high productivity and efficient quality control can be viewed firsthand on a tour of a Japanese factory. There is usually no fee, and often an English-speaking guide is available. A partial list of possible tours includes

> Toyota Motor Corporation
> Nissan Motor Company
> Toshiba Science Institute
> Tokyo National FA (Robot) Centre
> Suntory Brewery
> Asahi Newspaper
> Tokyo Stock Exchange
> NHK Broadcasting Centre

The NEC electronics corporation (located in front of the Uchisaiwaicho subway station) has a showroom open to the public from 10 am to 6 pm daily. Tokyo Central Wholesale Market is gigantic, selling fish, fruits, and vegetables. A three-hour tour is available from major hotels by Japan Gray Line, tel: (03) 433-5745.

The Japan Travel Bureau (JTB) offers a one-day 'Industrial Tokyo' tour which is probably the most worry-free and time-efficient way to get a glimpse of industrial Japan. For addresses of helpful business bureau and government agencies, see Appendix.

KYOTO

Overview

The Japanese think of Tokyo as Japan's head and Kyoto as its heart. As the country's capital for more than a thousand years, Kyoto has nurtured Japan's religious and cultural traditions: the Noh theatre, the tea ceremony, geisha entertainment. Its surrounding hills and distant mountains inspired painters and poets. Because Kyoto was one of the few areas spared by allied bombing attacks in World War Two it has more surviving landmarks than any other Japanese city — over one-fifth of the country's total — drawing twenty million visitors a year from the rest of Japan.

The majority of these landmarks are Buddhist temples and Shinto shrines that are still in use. Some are found in the very centre of the business district, where once-tranquil courtyards now serve as car parks. But the most noted ones are safely perched on nearby slopes, protected by parks. The inside of a temple compound looks as it did when the shoguns ruled feudal Japan; monks and worshippers carry out centuries-old rites.

Silks, porcelain, and lacquer are all produced in Kyoto, which is also the educational centre of western Japan. More than a thousand years ago, an early city planner laid the city streets out in grids. Despite all the inroads of modern expansion, this ancient symbol of Japanese culture remains to distinguish Kyoto as one of the world's truly fabulous cities.

Kyoto orientation

Kyoto is basically a rectangle with Kyoto station at the southern base. Anyone coming to the city by train or bus will arrive at Kyoto Station. In the middle of the city stands Nijo Castle and the old Imperial Palace. To the east of the palace are Kiyomizu ('clear water') Temple and the Silver Pavilion. To the west are Ryoanji, known for its rock garden, and the Golden Pavilion.

Existing side by side with modern industries is a thriving traditional crafts trade. Craftsmen's skills have been handed down through generations of families and are very much in evidence today in Kyoto and in many other historic cities, towns, and villages. The following is a partial listing of places in Kyoto where you can watch artists work. Admission is free unless otherwise indicated.

● **Yuzen Cultural Hall** is a five-minute walk from Kankyu Line's Nishi-Kogoku Station. The exhibit includes not only a beautiful collection of Yuzen kimoni; it also includes demonstrations of 300-year-old dyeing techniques used in making the kimono. Open daily from 9.00 am to 5.00 pm (last admission 4.00 pm). Admission Y300.

● **Kyoto Handicraft Centre**, a two-minute walk from Kumano-Jinja-mae bus stop, is a retail cooperative composed of Kyoto's leading craftsmen and handicraft shops. You can watch artists making pottery, silks, damascene, lacquerware, woodblock prints, dolls, etc. The Centre is open daily from 9.00 am to 6.00 pm.

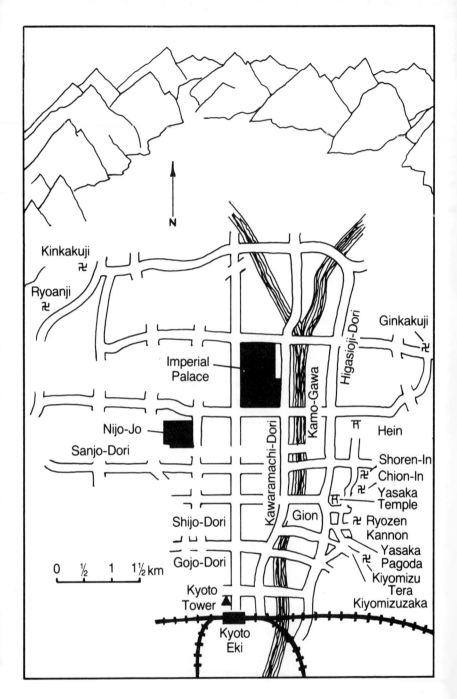

Map 4. Kyoto

124

● **Inaba Cloisonné**, a one-minute walk from Keihan Line's Sanjo Station, is a retailer/manufacturer of cloisonné (objects with fired enamel decoration) accessories and crafts. You can watch craftsmen at work and buy the finished products. Open daily from 9.00 am to 5.30 pm, the workshop is closed on Sundays and, in summer and winter, on the second Saturday of each month.

● **Kyoto Municipal Museum of Traditional Industry**, a one-minute walk from Kyoto-Kaika-Bijutudan-mae bus stop, not only exhibits various handicrafts made of silk, bamboo, lacquer, handmade paper, and ceramics; it also demonstrates the centuries-old production process of various handicrafts. The museum is open daily from 9.00 am to 5.00 pm except on Mondays.

Transport in Kyoto

Running from Kyoto Station in the south to Kitaoji in the north is Kyoto's one subway line. The best way to travel around Kyoto, however, is by bus. More than ten different bus routes begin at Kyoto Station, departing regularly for all parts of the city.

Kyoto is not a very large city, so if you have the time and the energy, you might choose to walk. Just get a map at the tourist information centre and explore. For the less adventurous guided tours are available.

Tourist information services in Kyoto

Japan Travel-phone is a service offering information in English. The telephone number for the Kyoto area is (075) 371-5649; hours are 9.00 am to 5.00 pm daily.

The **Kyoto Teletourist Service** is a 24-hour service which plays a 90-second tape in English describing events taking place during the coming week. The number is (075) 361-2911.

Three tourist offices in Kyoto offer information in English to visitors:

1. **The Kyoto Tourist Information Centre**, in the Kyoto Tower building, (075) 371-5649. The office is open from 9.00 am to 5.00 pm Monday through Friday, 9.00 am to noon on Saturday, and closed Sundays and holidays. The telephone service is available from 9.00 am to 5.00 pm daily.

2. **The Department of Cultural Affairs and Tourism**, Tourist Section, located at Kyoto Kaikan Okazaki, (075) 752-0215.

3.   **The Japan Travel Bureau**, directly outside the central exit of Tokyo Station.

OSAKA

Overview

Central Japan is known as the Kansai area, of which Osaka is the centre. A large city of over two and a half million people, Osaka lies at the mouth of the Shin-Yodo river, which empties into the Bay of Osaka. The city forms the heart of the Hanshin Industrial Zone. Laced with both natural and man-made canals, Osaka is known as the 'Venice of Japan' to some, and the place to make money to everyone. In former days people greeted each other with the phrase, 'How is business?' instead of 'Good morning.' When Tokyo was merely a fishing village, Osaka, blessed with extensive waterways and energetic merchants, was already an important commercial centre. The people of Osaka are considered to be aggressive, forward-looking, outspoken, and less self-conscious than the people of other areas in Japan. Their dialect (**Osaka-ben**) reflects this attitude. It is lively and emotional.

Osaka has a long and venerable history. In 1584 the great Osaka-Jo castle was built for the military ruler of the time; since then Osaka has been a centre for both domestic and foreign commerce as well as a transport and communications hub for the whole Kansai District.

Today, the Osaka area is a supercity, with Osaka functioning as the heart of a megalopolis that runs from Kyoto to Kobe and beyond. This area is said to account for more than 30 percent of Japan's industrial output, almost 40 percent of the nation's commercial and foreign trade transactions, and over 40 percent of its exports. Some 500,000 factories, large and small, are responsible for this output, most of it chemicals, heavy industry, textiles, food, and printing. Naturally, the result is smokestacks, crowded streets, pollution, and massive buildings. There is as little room for green parks and peace and quiet as in any other huge metropolis. Osaka is not a particularly beautiful city, but it is modern. Its driving energy and ancient culture make an exciting and pleasurable combination.

Osaka orientation

The city of Osaka can be a little confusing at first, but you can easily become familiar with its layout. It can be divided into three sections: north, central, and south. Two main boulevards run the length of the city. Traffic on Mido-suji runs from north to south, and traffic on Yotsubashi-suji runs south to north. These handsome avenues lined with gingko and other trees, banks, office buildings, and department stores are evidence of the city's prosperity.

The area around Osaka Station forms the heart of the northern part of the city. This area is called Umeda (plum field). Located here are the main post office, the Hankyu and Hanshin department stores, many office buildings, restaurants, and hotels. Here too is the city's main traffic hub, the terminal point for interurban buses and railway lines leading to outlying areas. The Umeda Underground Centre is a bustling market, lined with stores and cafes. The Shinchi area is well known for its posh, expensive restaurants.

Further to the north, across the Shin-Yodo river, is Shin-Osaka station, where the Shinkansen terminal is located. To the northwest lies Itami Airport (Osaka International Airport).

The central part of the city includes a large island called Nakano-shima, lying between the Dojima and Tosabori rivers. Here are situated the city offices, *Asahi* newspaper, part of Osaka University, the prefectural library, Nakanoshima Park, and many of the big hotels. To the east of Nakanoshima is the Osaka-Jo castle, destroyed and rebuilt several times over the centuries. The present building is five storeys high and made of reinforced concrete, a replica of the 1931 version. It stands high on a 46-foot rampart commanding a broad view of the city and its surroundings. It is brilliantly illuminated at night and visible for miles. In this area the Osaka immigration office and police headquarters are also based.

The southern part of the city is the area around Namba Station. This is Osaka's entertainment district, including the huge Shin-Kabukiza Theatre; the Bunraku Puppet Theatre; and Dotobori, a street of small theatres and restaurants along the Shirinashi River. There are also many music halls, cabarets, cinemas, stores, and bars. The covered, pedestrian shopping street of Shinsaibashi-siji is a wonderful place to spend the day walking and window-shopping.

Top the southeast of Namba is the area called Tennoji, a pleasant area of the city, with a botanical garden and a large park. The Tennoji Zoo is a great place to take the children for a day (try to avoid Sunday when it is quite crowded). The Shitennoji Temple, with its aura of ancient Japan, is also in this area.

Outside the city a substantial mountain range extends over Nara and Osaka prefectures, and a sixty-square-mile park has been established for hiking, camping, and other recreation. Mt. Ikoma in the north rises over 22,000 feet and is reached by cable car or the Hannan Highway; there are large and lovely recreation areas at the top and a spectacular view. In the west, at the Osaka Ferry Terminal, ferries leave daily for Kyushu

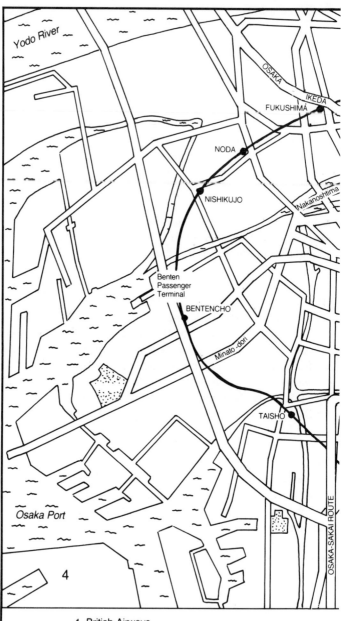

1. British Airways
2. Osaka Chamber of Commerce and Industry
3. Foreign Trade Institute
4. INTEX OSAKA (International Exhibition Center)
5. Osaka University Hospital
6. Bank of Japan
7. Bank of America
8. Sanwa Bank
9. Hong-Kong and Shanghai Bank

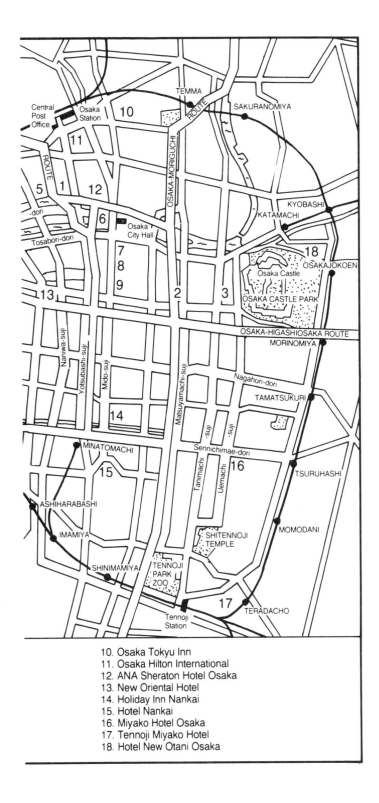

10. Osaka Tokyu Inn
11. Osaka Hilton International
12. ANA Sheraton Hotel Osaka
13. New Oriental Hotel
14. Holiday Inn Nankai
15. Hotel Nankai
16. Miyako Hotel Osaka
17. Tennoji Miyako Hotel
18. Hotel New Otani Osaka

and other parts of Japan and offer a different way to view the country.

This is the best city in which to visit industries and observe Japanese production methods. Twenty-three companies of all kinds — cars, beer, TVs, vitamins, electronics computers, diesel engines, farm machines — offer tours through the Osaka City Office and Osaka Tourist Association. If you are interested, inquire through your hotel, the Japan Travel Bureau (JTB), the Trade and Tourist Section of the Economic Bureau in Osaka (1-4 Nakanoshima, Kita-ku), or the Osaka Tourist Association office in Osaka Station.

Of particular interest is the Osaka International Trade Centre, a permanent trade show of twenty thousand products from approximately five hundred companies throughout Japan. Visiting businesspeople are provided whatever information, guidance, and contacts they need. Appointments and consultations are readily arranged, and all of it is free. The Trade Centre is near the New Osaka Hotel at 2, 2-chome, Tamai-cho, Kita-ku.

Getting around

Getting a taxi in the business area is not always easy, and in the rain or during rush hours it is virtually impossible unless you order it ahead. Osaka cabbies are tough and will often turn down a short ride. In the Umeda and Nakanoshima areas it is quicker to walk or take a train. The JR trains run all around the city in a loop, from Osaka Station to Osaka Bay, to Tennoji, to Osaka Castle and on. As in Tokyo, the trains ring the city, while the subways go through the middle. The Midosuji line runs from Shin-Osaka through Umeda to Namba and Tennoji. The Chuo line runs east to west, and numerous others run to most other areas in the city. Trains and subways run every three minutes or so from about 5.30 am to midnight.

Buses are another option. As in Tokyo all bus routes are in Japanese, so the same advice will be helpful: if you must take a bus, have your destination written down in Japanese and ask the bus driver if the bus goes where you want to go. Usually the drivers are very kind and will tell you when your stop comes up.

Tourist information services in Osaka

Japan Travel-phone is a service offering information in English. The telephone number for the Kansai area is (0120) 444-8000. Hours are 9.00 am to 5.00 pm daily.

Osaka's tourist industry includes three separate tourist agencies that provide English-speaking service to foreign visitors and guests.

Osaka Tourist Association
The Osaka municipal tourist offices operates three offices, providing many services in English:

- Osaka Tourist Information Centre, at Shin-Osaka station (east side of the central gate). Tel: (06) 305-3311. 8.00 am - 8.00 pm daily.

- Osaka Tourist Information Office, at JR Osaka Station (east side of the east gate). Tel: (06) 345-2189. 8.00 am - 7.00 pm daily.

- Osaka Castle Information Centre, Main Keep (first floor). Tel: (06) 944-0546. 9.00 am - 5.00 pm daily.

Osaka Tourist Information Service
Located in the International Hotel lobby. Tel: (06) 941-9200. Noon - 7.00 pm daily; closed Tuesdays.

Japan Travel Bureau (JTB)
Has desks in Osaka Station, the New Osaka Hotel, Osaka Grand Hotel, and the Asahi Building. Tel: (06) 341-5006. JTB also maintains the Foreigner Office, which provides many services in English for travellers. It is near Higobashi Station on the Yotsubashi subway line. Tel: (06) 449-1071.

KOBE

Overview
Thirty-one percent of Japan's exports pass through Kobe Harbour, and at least nine thousand ships call at its port each year. The port dates back to the third century, when the culture of China and Korea began to flow into Japan. Post activity stretches some eighteen miles east and west along the Bay of Osaka. This is an area of heavy industry — steel, shipbuilding, railroad stock — as well as such light industries as food processing, rubber, and vinyl manufacturing. Commercial activity, both domestic and foreign, is brisk. Out of some 1,300,000 residents, 30,000 are foreigners.

Outside the industrial area, Kobe is full of interesting and scenic places. The Rokko Mountain Range, various lovely beaches, and the Arima Hot Springs are close at hand; there are drives, parks, waterfalls, cable cars, boat excursions, temples, observation points, and recreation complexes; and Kyoto, Nara, and Osaka are within easy range.

The Rokko Mountains, stretching twenty-four miles from east to west behind the city, shield it from strong north winds in the winter, keeping the temperature far more pleasant than it would otherwise be. Mt Rokko itself, the highest peak, is about three thousand feet; Mt Maya, second highest, about two thousand. Cable cars carry passengers to the top, or one can drive up as well. At the northern end of Rokko, along a gorge, are some thirty small inns, each with its own medicinal hot spring bath.

To the west of the city lie the white sands and dark pines of Suma and Maiko beaches, near the entry to the Inland Sea. Anyone based in this area will find plenty to do and beautiful surroundings.

Kobe orientation

The centre of Kobe is the area around Sannomiya Station on the JR Tokaido line. North of Sannomiya is Shin-Kobe Station, where the Shinkansen terminal is located. North of Shin-Kobe are the Rokko Mountains. The southern part of Kobe is the port. A large island extends out into the port (Port Island), where there are many fashion-related industries as well as Kobe International Exhibition Hall, the Conference Centre, the Science Museum, and Portopia Lan (a large amusement park). Just east of Kobe lies the famous Himeji Castle. Also known as the White Heron Castle, it is the one most often featured in books about Japan.

Getting around Kobe

The JR Tokaido subway line runs the length of Kobe, with lines branching off from Sannomiya Station. A monorail called the Port Lines, goes to Port Island. Taxis are plentiful, and there are many car hire agencies. The boarding point for the bus to Osaka Airport is at Sannomiya Station in front of the JAL office.

Tourist information services in Kobe

Japan Travel-phone service offers information in English. The Telephone number for the Kobe area is (0120) 444-8000.

The Kobe House and Information Centre, at 6-15 Ikuta-cho, Chuo-ku, is an information service for foreigners about hotels, hospitals, etc., in the Kobe area. Tel: (078) 242-1043.

A Japanese Glossary

GREETINGS AND COURTESIES

Ohio gozaimasu	Good morning
Konichi wa	Good day
Kon ban wa	Good evening
Oyasuminasai	Good night
Hajimemashite	How do you do
Yoroshiku	Pleased to meet you
Sayonara	Goodbye
Domo	Thanks
Arigato	Thank you
Domo arigato gozaimashita	Thank you very much
Kudasai	Please
Onegai shimasu	Please do me a favour. . .
Sore ja, mata ne	See you later
Gomen nasai (or) **Sumimasen**	Excuse me
Shitsurei shimasu (or) **O jama shimashita**	I've been rude, imposed on you

COUNTRIES AND LANGUAGES

Nihon	Japan
Nihongo	Japanese (language)
Eikoko	England
Eigo	English (language)
Eigo ga dekimasuka?	Can you speak English?
Nihongo ga dekimasuka?	Can you speak Japanese?
Hai dekimaso	Yes I can.
Iie, Nihongo ga dekimasen.	No, I can't speak Japanese.

133

TIMES

The day

asa	morning
hiru	afternoon
yube	evening
yoru	night
kesa	this morning
kiyo	today
konban	tonight
ima	now
ato de	later
mae ni	before
kino	yesterday
ashita	tomorrow
asatte	day after tomorrow
ototoi	day before yesterday

The week

Nichiyobi	Sunday
Getsuyobi	Monday
Kayobi	Tuesday
Suiyobi	Wednesday
Mokuyobi	Thursday
Kinyobi	Friday
Doyobi	Saturday

The year

kotoshi	this year
rainen	next year
kyonen	last year
haru	spring
natsu	summer
aki	autumn
fuyu	winter
iichigatsu	January
nigatsu	February
sangatsu	March
shigatsu	April
gogatsu	May
rokugatsu	June

shichigatsu	July
hachigatsu	August
kugatsu	September
jugatsu	October
juiichigatsu	November
junigatsu	December

GETTING AROUND

densha	train
Shinkansen	high-speed train
chikatetsu	subway
aruite	walk
takushi	taxi
hikoki	plane
basu	bus
fune	boat
kuruma (or) jidosha	car

Where is. . .?

Doko desuka	Where is. . .?
Toirei wa doko desuka?	Where is the toilet?
Eki wa doko desuka?	Where is the station?
Keisatsu wa doko desuka?	Where is the policeman?
Oteru wa doko desuka?	Where is a hotel?
Ginko wa doko desuka?	Where is a bank?
Basu tei wa doko desuka?	Where is the bus stop?

Which way. . .?

migi	right
hidari	left
mae ri	in front of
ushiro ni	behind
kita	north
minami	south
nishi	west
higashi	east
kaidan	stairs
erebeta	lift
ue	up
shita	down

chickai/toi	near/far

Places

machi	town
shi	city
doro	road
wan	bay
shima	island
yama	mountain
kawa	river
hanto	peninsula
zaki	cape

ACCOMMODATION

oteru	hotel
minshuku	minshuku
ryokan	ryokan
heya	room
toirei	toilet
o-furo	bath
Nihon shoku	Japanese food
yushoku	western food
tauru	towel
suripa	slippers
washitsu	Japanese room
yoshitsu	western-style room
nishoku	room w/two meals
ryokin	room charge
yoyaku	reservation
Ikura desuka?	How much?
Heya ga arimasuka?	Do you have a room?
Hai, heya ga arimasu.	Yes, we do.
Iie, heya ga arimasen.	We have no room.

HEALTH

tetsudaite kudasai	please help me
isha (or) sensei	doctor
kusuriya	chemist
kusuri	medicine

byooin	hospital
kyukyusha	ambulance
itai	hurt(s)
byoki	sick
atama ga itai	headache
onaka ga itai	stomach ache
nodo ga itai	sore throat
karada	body
me	eye
mimi	ear
hana	nose
kuchi	mouth
ude	arm
ashi	leg

GENERAL

denwa	telephone
kokusai denwa	international telephone
chotto matte	just a moment
ano ne!	hey!
subarashi	wonderful
sugoi	great!
ipai/suite imasu	full/empty
yopparai	drunk
shiawase/sabishi	happy/sad
genki	healthy
ii/dame	good/bad
oishi/mazui	delicious/tasteless
okii/chisai	big/small
nagai/michikai	long/short
semai/hiroi	narrow/wide
ai/kirai	love/hate
yasui/takai	cheap/expensive
kirei	beautiful
haiyai/yukuri	fast/slow
atsui/samui	hot/cold
nemuri	sleep
Nemutai	I want to sleep
mise	shop
hakubutsukan	museum

hon ya san	bookshop
shokudo	restaurant

EXECUTIVES OF ORGANISATIONS

Kaicho	Chairman
Shacho	President
Fuku-Shacho	Vice President
Senmu-Torishimariyaku	Senior Executive Managing Director
Jomu-Torishimariyaku	Executive Managing Director
Torishimariyaku	Director
Bucho	Divisional Manager
Bucho Dairi	Deputy Divisional Manager
Kacho	Section Manager (Section Chief)
Kacho Dairi	Deputy Section Manager
Kakaricho	Chief

FOOD

Onaka suita	I'm hungry
Nodo ga itai	I'm thirsty
Onaka ipai	I'm full up
o-hashi	chopsticks
amai	sweet
Supai	sour
karai	spicy hot
nigai	bitter
aji	flavour
atsui	hot
sumetai	cold (food or drink)
oishi	delicious
sugoku oishi	very delicious

Meat and rice

o-ohan	rice, or food in general
nikku	meat (usually beef)
bekon	bacon
hamu	ham
buta nikku	pork
tori	chicken (bird)

Seafood

o-sushi	sushi
sakana	fish
kani	crab
ebi	shrimp
oki ebi	lobster
hammachi	yellow tail
kaki	oysters
hamaguri	clam
unagi	eel
uni	sea urchin
ikka	squid
maguro	tuna

Sauces

wasabi	horseradish mustard
o-shoyu	soy sauce
sosu	Japanese sauce with ketchup and Worcester sauce

Fruit and vegetables

retasu	lettuce
kinoko	mushroom
shitake	a fine white mushroom
kabetsu	cabbage
take no ko	bamboo shoots
ninjin	carrot
jagaimo	potato
ninnikku	garlic
remon	lemon
meron	melon
ringo	apple
orenji	orange
mikan	Japanese orange
ichigo	strawberry

Breakfast

pan	bread
tamago	eggs
bata	butter
tosto	toast

jamu	jam
sato	sugar

Beverages

Kora	cola
o-mizu	water
sumetai mizu	cold water
o-yu	hot water
o-cha	green tea
ban-cha	tea made with roasted rice
ko-cha	Chinese tea (with caffeine)
miruku	milk
kurimu	cream
jusu	juice
beeru	beer
o-sake	liquor, rice wine
wainu	wine
mizu wari	scotch and water
sho chu	rice spirits
shochu remon	shochu cocktail, lemony
masu zake	cold sake in a cedar box

Food talk

Kore wa nana desuka?	What is this?
Kore wa Gohan desu.	This is rice.
Ii desuka?	Is it all right?
Hai, ii desu.	Yes, it is.
Kampai!	Cheers!
oishi (desu)	delicious, (it's) delicious
dozo	please have some
domo	thank you
kekko desu	that's fine (enough), thank you.
Gochiso-sama deshita	I enjoyed that/it was really delicious
Tempura soba kudasai.	Tempura noodles, please.
Ramen soba kudasai	Ramen noodles, please.
Kohii kudasai	Coffee, please.

Useful Addresses

EMBASSIES & GOVERNMENT OFFICES

Japanese Embassy, 46 Grosvenor Street, London W1. Tel: (071) 493 6030.

Japanese Consular Visa Section, 101 Picadilly, London W1. Tel: (071) 464 6500.

British Embassy in Tokyo, No 1 Ichibancho 1-chome, Chiyoda-ku, Tokyo 102.

British Council in Tokyo, 2 Kagurazaka 1-chome, Shinkuku-ku, Tokyo 162.

Immigration offices in Japan

Tokyo Immigration office, No 1 Ohtemachi Godochosha, 3-1 Ohtemachi 1-chome, Chiyoda-ku, Tokyo 100. Tel: (03) 213-8111.

Kobe Immigration Office, Kobe Chiho Godochosha, Kaigan-dori, Chuo-ku. Tel: (078) 391 6377/9.

Osaka Immigration Office, No 2 Homu Godochosha, 31 Tani-machi 2-chome, Higashi-ku. Tel: (06) 941 0771/5.

Yokohama Immigration Office, 37-9 Yamashita-cho, Naka-ku. Tel: (045) 681-6801/4.

INTERNATIONAL SOCIETIES

In London

Japan Society of London, 168 Regent Street, London W1. Tel: (071) 434 4507.

Women's Corona Society, Room 501 Eland House, Stag Place, London SW1E 5DE. Tel: (071) 828 1652/3. Exists to promote knowledge and understanding of the peoples and cultures of the world and to provide advice to women going to live temporarily in another country. Runs one day courses in London, plus talks, and postal courses.

In Japan

Japan-British Society, Tokyo Building, 7-3 Marunouchi 2-chome, Chiyoda -ku, Tokyo. Tel: (03) 211 8027. The counterpart of the Japan Society of London. Founded in 1908 to promote the study of things British in Japan.

BUSINESS CONTACTS

United Kingdom

Anglo-Japanese Economic Institute, 342/6 Grand buildings, Trafalgar Square, London WC2N 5HB. Tel: (071) 930 5567. Established in 1961 by the Japanese Embassy in London. It publishes a bulletin on Anglo-Japanese relations and maintains a library.

British Overseas Trade Board (BOTB), Export Services and Promotion Division, Export House, 50 Ludgate Hill, London EC4M 7HU. Tel: (071) 248 5757. Provides a range of information on how to do business in Japan, from business methods to documentation, market research, agency and other business services.

Exports to Japan Unit (EJU), Department of Trade & Industry, 66-74 Victoria Street, London SW1E 6SW. Tel: (071) 215 4804. Produces a number of published guides and provides information and advice for intending exporters to Japan.

Japan Agency & Consultancy, 348 Regent's Park Road, London N3. Tel: (081) 349 0011.

Japan Association, 43-46 King William Street, London EC4R 9BE.

Japan Business Consultancy, Newton Park, Bath, Avon BA1 9BN. Tel: (0225) 874146.

Japan Centre, 66 Brewer Street, London W1R 3PJ. Tel: (071) 439 8035. Specialist in books on Japan and in Japanese.

Japan Foundation, 35 Dover Street, London W1. Tel: (071) 499 4726.

Japan International Bank Ltd, 107 Cheapside, London EC2. Tel: (071) 600 0931.

Japan Productivity Centre, 20 Rupert Street, London W1. Tel: (071) 734 0317.

Japan Trade Centre, 6th Floor, Leconfield House, Curzon Street, London W1Y 6FB. Tel: (071) 493 7226.

Japanese Chamber of Commerce & Industry, 2nd floor, Salisbury House, 29 Finsbury Circus, London EC2M 5QQ. Tel: (071) 628 0069.

JETRO (Japan External Trade Organisation). Based at the Japan Trade Centre (see above).

University of Sheffield Japan Business Services Unit, Sheffield S10

2TN. Tel: (0742) 78555. Provides individual and group courses for companies and private individuals planning to take up residence in Japan.

Business contacts in Japan

American Chamber of Commerce, 7F Fukide Daini building, 4-1-4 Toranomon, Minato-ku, Tokyo. Tel: (03) 3433-5381.

Association of Management Consultants in Japan, Shuwa Shiba Koen, 3-chome Building, 1-38 Shiba Koen 3-chome, Minato-ku, Tokyo 105. Tel: (03) 3436-2085.

British Chamber of Commerce in Japan (BCCJ), PO Box 2145, World Import Mart Branch, Toshima-ku, Tokyo 170.

Japan American Society, Room 370, Marunouchi Building, 2-4-1 Marunouchi, Chiyoda-ku, Tokyo 100. Tel: (03) 3201-0780.

Japan Chamber of Commerce & Industry, 2-2, 3-chome Marunouchi, Chiyoda-ku, Tokyo 100. Tel: (03) 3283 7867.

Japan External Trade Organisation (JETRO), 2-5, Toranomon 2-chome, Minato-ku, Tokyo 107. Also offices in London. Japanese government organisation established to promote exports.

Japan International Trade Promotion Organisation (JITPA), Nippon Building, 5th floor, 2-6-2, Ohtemachi, Chiyoda-ku, Tokyo. Tel: (03) 3216-1901.

Tokyo International Trade Fair Commission, 7-24 Harumi 4-chome, Chuo-ku, Tokyo. Tel: (03) 3531-3371.

US Trade Center, 7th floor, World Import Mart Building, 3-1-3 Higashi-Ikebukuro, Toshima-ku, Tokyo. Tel: (03) 3987-2441.

CULTURAL & EDUCATIONAL CONTACTS

In the United Kingdom

British Library, Japanese Information Services, 25 Southampton Buildings, London WC2A 1AW. Tel: (071) 323 7924.

Centre for International Briefing, Farnham Castle, Farnham, Surrey GU9 0AG. Runs 4 to 5 day residential courses for people going to work overseas. Can assist with financial planning. Includes a bookshop. The Centre is used by a large number of international firms and organisations.

Centre for Japanese Studies, University of Sheffield, Sheffield S10 2NT. Tel: (0742) 78555.

Centre for Japanese Studies, University of Stirling, Scotland FK9 4LA. Tel: (0786) 3171.

Centre for the Study of Contemporary Japan, Essex University, Wivehoe Park, Colchester CO4 3SQ. Tel: (0206) 862286.

Euro-Japanese Exchange Foundation (EJEF), Lane End, nr High Wycombe, Buckinghamshire. Tel: (0494) 882091. Runs courses in Japanese language from elementary to advanced levels, plus business orientation and other courses.

Japanese School Ltd, 17 Mayfield Road, London W3. Tel: (081) 993 7145.

In Japan

American Center Library, 11th Floor, ABC Kaikan Building, 2-6-3 Shibakoen, Minato-ku, Tokyo. Tel: (03) 3436 0901.

American Club, 2-1-2 Asabudai, Minato-ku, Tokyo. Tel: (03) 3583 8381.

EMPLOYMENT OPPORTUNITIES IN JAPAN

Japan Recruitment, Plantation House, Fenchurch Street, London EC3. Tel: (071) 621 0648. Also: 5 Sherwood Street, London W1V 7RA. Tel: (071) 4421/4422.

Japan Services Employment, Employment Agency for Japanese Speakers, 18 Warwick Street, London W1. Tel: (071) 439 6452.

Anglo-Japanese Agency (Recruitment & Employment Services), 23 Wormwood Street, London EC2. Tel: (071) 256 9371.

JAPANESE GOODS & SERVICES

Japan Animal Welfare Society, RMC House, Townmead Road, London SW6. Tel: (072) 836 9306.

Japan England International Services Ltd. Staple Hall, Stonehouse Court, London EC3. Tel: (071) 929 3656.

Japan Letting Agency, Lamerton House, High Street, London W5. Tel: (081) 567 3360.

Japan Print Gallery (fine Japanese prints), 43 Pembridge Road, London W11. Tel: (071) 221 0927.

Japan Video, 4 Monkville Parade, Finchley Road, London NW11. Tel: (081) 455 8811.

Japanese Gallery (commissions, valuations, estimates), 66d Kensington Church Street, London W8. Tel: (071) 229 2934.

Japanese Hairdressers Baron Yoshimoto, 104 St John's Wood Terrace, London NW8. Tel: (071) 722 6970.

Japanese Shop Mitsukiku Ltd, 15 Old Brompton Road, London SW7. Tel: (071) 589 1725. Has several London branches.

JAPANESE RESTAURANTS IN LONDON

Japanese Restaurant, 9 Dicey Avenue, London NW2. Tel: (081) 452 7513.
Japanese Restaurant Masako, 6 St Christopher's Place, London W1. Tel: (071) 486 1399.
Japanese Restaurant Miyama, 38 Clarges Street, London W1. Tel: (071) 499 2443.
Japanese Restaurant One, Two, Three, 27 Davies Street, London W1. Tel: (071) 491 1310.

MOTORING INFORMATION

In the United Kingdom
Japan Car Hire, 72 Pancras Road, London NW1. Tel: (071) 383 7481.
Japan & Europe Motors, 46 Watford Way, London NW4. Tel: (081) 202 2522.
Japan Executive Chauffeurs, 97a Victoria Road, London NW6. Tel: (071) 624 4623.
Nissan UK Press & PR Office, 5 Arlington Street, London SW1. Tel: (071) 493 3088.
Toyota (GB) Ltd, The Quadrangle, Redhill, Surrey. Tel: Redhill 768565.
Automobile Association, Fanum House, PO Box 118, Park Row, Bristol BS99 7XZ.
Department of Transport, 2 Marsham Street, London SW1. Tel: (071) 276 3000.

In Japan
Avis-Nissan Rent-a-Car, Landick Iikura Building (6th floor), 5-6 Azabu-dai 1-chome, Minato-ku, Tokyo. Tel: (03) 595 9895.
Hertz-Nippon Rent-a-Car, Jinnan Building, 4-3 Udagawa-cho, Shibuya-ku, Tokyo. Tel: (03) 469 0910 or 499 3627.
Licensing Offices. Samezu Office, 12-5 Higashi-oi 1 -chome, Shinaga-wa-ku, Tokyo. Tel: (03) 474 1274. Fuchu Office, 1-1 Tamamachi 3-chome, Fuchu, Tokyo. Tel: (0423) 62 3591.

JAPANESE MEDIA

In the United Kingdom
Japanese Daily Newspaper, 12 Norwich Street, London EC4. Tel: (071) 353 8301.

Japan Financial News Company Ltd, Redhill Terrace, 4 Oakley Avenue, London W5 3SA. Tel: (081) 992 4643.

Japan Journals Ltd, 52 Haymarket, London SW1. Tel: (071) 839 7277.

Japan Radio Co Ltd, 194 Temple Chambers, London EC4. Tel: (071) 353 7960.

In Japan

Foreign Correspondents Club of Japan, 20th Floor, Yurakucho Denki Building, Kita-kan 7-1, Yuraku-cho 1-chome, Chiyoda-ku, Tokyo 100. Tel: (03) 3211-3161.

Foreign Press Centre, 6th Floor, Nippon Press Centre Building, 2-1 Uchisaiwai-cho 2-chome, Chiyoda-ku, Tokyo 100. Tel: (03) 3501 4301.

TRANSLATING & INTERPRETERS

Japan Press & Language Services, 39 Farringdon Road, London EC1. Tel: (071) 242 5659.

Japaneeds (Multilingua) Ltd, 11 Uxbridge Street, London W8. Tel: (071) 229 7231.

Japanese Translations Interpreting, 4/7 Lyncroft Gardens, London NW6. Tel: (071) 435 2566.

Japanese College of Languages, la Wilson Street, London N21. Tel: (081) 886 6434.

Japanese Commercial & Technical Translations, Marzell House, 116 North End Road, London W14. Tel: (071) 381 0967.

Japanese Conversation Club, London SW10. Tel: (071) 352 7716.

Japanese Guiding & Interpreting Bureau. As above.

Japanese Interpreting & Translation Services, 4/15 Belsize Park Gardens, London NW3. Tel: (071) 722 2080.

Japanese Technical Translation Company, 76 Shoe Lane, London EC4. Tel: (071) 583 8690.

Japanese Technical Translation & Print, Alpha House, 74 Maida Vale, London W9. Tel: (071) 624 2525.

Japanese Technological Translations, 17 Nightingale Centre, Balham Hill, London SW12. Tel: (081) 673 0865.

Japanese Translation & Print, 10 St Cross Street, London EC1. Tel: (071) 405 2202.

Japanese Translations, 64 Queen Street, London EC4. Tel: (071) 248 8707.

Japanese Translation & Typesetting, Berkeley Square House, Berkeley Square, London W1. Tel: (071) 409 0953.

TRAVEL AND TOURISM

In the United Kingdom

Anglo-Japanese Travel Service, 20 Rupert Street, London W1. Tel: (071) 437 8277.

Japan Airlines (JAL), 5 Hanover Square, London W1. Tel: (071) 629 9244.

Japan Business Travel (UK) Ltd, 27 New Bond Street, London W1. Tel: (071) 629 8356.

Japan Executive Travel, 48 Brewer Street, London W1. Tel: (071) 439 3601.

Japan National Tourist Organisation (JNTO), 167 Regent Street, London W1 3DD. Tel: (071) 734 9638.

Japan Travel Bureau (JTB), 10 Maltravers Street, London WC2. Tel: (071) 379 6244. Also: 190 Strand, London WC2. Tel: (071) 836 9367.

Japan Travel Centre, 66 Brewer Street, London W1. Tel: (071) 437 6445.

Japanese Travel Centre, 5 Sherwood Street, London W11. Tel: (071) 287 0838.

In Japan

Japan National Tourist Organisation (JNTO), Tokyo Kotsu Kaikan Building, 2-10-1, Yuraku-cho, Chiyoda-ku, Tokyo. Tel: (03) 3216 1901.

Japan Travel Bureau (JTB), Foreign Tourists Department, Nittetsu Nihonbashi Building, 13-1 Nihonbashi 1-chome, Chuo-ku, Tokyo 102. Tel: (03) 276 7777. Branches in many major towns and hotels.

Japan Youth Hostel Inc. Hoken Kaikan, 2 Ichigaya Sadohara-cho 1-chome, Shinjuku-ku, Tokyo 162. Tel: (03) 3269 5831.

Tourist Information Centre (TIC), 6-6 Yurakucho 1-chome, Chiyoda-ku, Tokyo 100. Tel: (03) 502 1461.

YMCA, 7 Kanda Mitoshiro-cho, Chiyoda-ku, Tokyo 101. Tel: (03) 3293 5421.

YWCA, 8-11 Kanda Surugadai 1-chome, Chiyoda-ku, Tokyo 101. Tel: (03) 3293 5421.

BRITISH LAWYERS SPECIALISING IN JAPAN

Baker & McKenzie, Aldwych House, Aldwych, London WC2B 4JP. Tel: (071) 242 6531. contact Mr P E Rood (Senior Partner). Can offer advice on Japanese tax, company and employment law.

Clifford Chance, Blackfriars House, 19 New Bridge Street, London EC4V 6BY. Tel: (071) 353 0211. Contact Mr A Jones (Assistant solicitor) for advice on Japanese law.

Denton Hall Burgin & Warrens, Denning House, 90 Chancery Lane, London WC2A 1EU. Tel: (071) 242 1212. Contact Mr C Clarke or Mr P Goodwin (Partners). International law practice with partners in London and the Far East offering advice on the Japanese and business in Japan and having a range of professional and business contacts in Japan.

Linklaters & Paines, Barrington House, 59-67 Gresham Street, London EC2V 7JA. Tel: (071) 606 7080/5113. Contact Mr C Allen-Jones (UK-based Partner) or Mr A Grundy (Tokyo-based Partner). Leading English law firm with an international practice offering a range of legal services. They opened their Tokyo office in 1988. Extensive commercial/corporate experience.

McKenna & Co, Inveresk House, 1 Aldwych, London WC2R 0HF. Tel: (071) 836 2442. Contacts: Mr J M H Bellhouse (Partner, Construction) or Mr R J Williams (Partner, Corporate). Specialising in corporate, financial, banking, company, commercial, property and construction law with offices in Tokyo, Hong Kong, Singapore and elsewhere. They have a Japanese desk in London staffed by Japanese speakers.

Richards Butler, 5 Clifton Street, London EC2A 4DQ. Tel: (071) 247 6555. Contact: Mr G Bowtle (Partner). Established London-based firm, with a Tokyo office staffed by two British partners. Coverage: aviation, shipping, international asset and project finance, merger and competition law, licensing, intellectual property and EC law.

Simmons & Simmons, 14 Dominion Street, London EC2M 2RJ. Tel: (071) 628 2020. Contact: Mr P de Chazal (Partner). Has links with professional firms in Japan and maintains an office in Hong Kong. Covers a wide commercial field including joint ventures, licensing and technical cooperation, distribution, agency, franchising and other aspects for pharmaceuticals, petrochemical, aerospace, brewing, engineering, satellite communications, motor, food and drinks and other industries.

Slaughter & May, 35 Basinghall Street, London EC2V 5DB. Tel: (071) 600 1200. Contact: Mr R M G Goulding (Partner). Established leading firm of solicitors, with an office in Tokyo.

Waterhouse & Co, 4 St Paul's Churchyard, London EC4M 8BA. Tel: (071) 236 2333. Contacts: Mr J Wilson or Mr J Facer (Partners). Offers Japanese connections with Japanese head offices, of various industrial and commercial companies, financial institutions, security houses etc. Has established contacts with Japanese law firms and legal departments.

Further Reading

MAPS & GUIDEBOOKS

Around Tokyo: A Day Tripper's Guide (2 vols), by John Turrent and
   Jonathan Lloyd-Owen (The Japan Times).
Exploring Kamakura, Michael Cooper (Weatherhill).
Exploring Tohuku, Jan Brown (Weatherhill).
Fodor's Japan and *Fodor's Budget Japan*, ed. Vivienne Kenrick (Fodor's
   Tavel Guides).
Footlose in Tokyo and *More Footlose in Tokyo*, Jean Pearce (Weatherhill).
Gaijin's Guide: Practical Help for Everyday Life in Japan, Janet Ashley
   (The Japan Times).
Good Tokyo Restaurants, R Kennedy (Kodansha). A useful guide, with
   maps.
Great Tokyo Detailed Map (Nippon Kukoseisho). Shows subway and bus
   routes, expressways, railways, leading stores and tourist sights.
Guide to Japanese Museums, Laurence Roberts (Weatherhill).
Handy Map of Tokyo (Japan Guide Map Co). Includes a good train map.
Insider's Guide to Japan, P Popham (Kodansha).
Japan Handbook, J D Bisignani (Moon Publications/Roger Lascelles,
   London).
Japan in your Pocket, David Old (Horizon Books). With suggested
   itineraries and numerous sketch maps.
Japan Solo, Eiji Kanno (Nitchi Map Publishing).
Japan Travel Survival Kit, Ian McQueen (Lonely Planet Publications).
Kanazawa, Ruth Stevens (Society to Introduce Kanazawa to the World).
Kyoto: A Contemplative Guide, Gouverneur Mosher (Tuttle).
Living in Kobe (CHIC). Essential reading for the Kansai resident.
Living in Tokyo, Tokyo Metropolitan Government (The Japan Times).
   Free from local Ward offices.
New Japan Solo, Kanno and O Keefe (Kodansha).

Now You Live in Japan, Research Committee for Bicultural Life (The Japan Times).

Tokyo Access, R S Wurnam (Access Press). Colour guide arranged by area, with text in English and Japanese.

Tokyo: Bilingual Atlas (Kodansha). With maps in English and Japanese.

Tokyo Transit, Gary Bassin (The Japan Times). Pocket guide to Tokyo's subway and train network.

Tourist Map of Tokyo (TIC). Free from TIC desks.

Yokohama My City (Japan Telecommunications Association). Comprehensive municipal guide.

TELECOMMUNICATIONS

Japan Times Directory: Foreign Residents, Business Firms and Organisations.

Japan Times Telephone Directory (The Japan Times).

Japan Yellow Pages. Phone (03) 239 3501.

PERIODICALS

Forecasts. Published six times a year, with news of forthcoming international arts events. International Music & Arts Service, 21-2 Nishi Azabu 2-chome, Minato-ku, Tokyo 106.

Japan Times. Leading newspaper. Japan Times, 5-4 2-cheni, Hirakawacho, Chiyoda-ku, Tokyo 10.

Japan Times Weekly, 5-4 Shibaura 4-chome, Minato-ku, Tokyo 108.

Kansai Time Out. A comprehensive what's on guide.

Mainichi Daily News, 1-1-1 Hitosubashi, Chiyoda-ku, Tokyo 100.

Shushoku Joho. A job magazine for Japanese studying in Europe and for Japanese-speakers in Europe. Available through: Recruit Europe Ltd, Berkeley Square House, Berkeley Square, London W1X 5LB. Tel: (071) 495 3929.

Tokyo Journal. A monthly magazine with articles on Japanese culture and travel, plus an extensive entertainments guide. Available from book stores, or on subscription from International Marketing Corporation, No5 Wako Bldg, 19-8 Kakigaracho 1-chome, Nihonbashi, Chuo-ku, Tokyo 103.

Tokyo Weekender. A weekly giveaway featuring events of interest to the foreign community. It has a useful classified section which is often used by expats. You can pick it up in supermarkets, hotels, and a variety of other locations around town.

Tour Companion. Another free weekly aimed mainly at tourists and listing details of the week's entertainments and festivals. It, too, is available in hotels and so on. There is a similar publication for the Kyoto/Osaka area.

BUSINESS

Business Guide to Japan, World of Information (Longman 1986). 63pp, map.

The Financial Development of Japan 1868 to 1977, Raymond Goldsmith (Yale University Press 1983).

Inside Japan's Financial Markets (Hodder 1988).

Japan, Economist Business Travellers Guides (The Economist/Collins 1987).

Japanese Banking and Capital Markets, Banker Research Unit (Financial Times Business Publications 1981).

Japanese Finance: A Guide to Banking in Japan, Andreas Prindl (Wiley 1981).

Japanese Financial Markets: Deficits, Dilemmas and Deregulations, Robert Alan Feldman (MIT Press 1986).

Japan's Financial Markets: Conflicts and Consensus in Policy Making, James Horne (Allen & Unwin/Australia Japan Research Centre 1985).

The Japanese Financial System, Yoshio Suzuki (Clarendon Press 1987).

The Japanese Money Market, Robert Emery (Lexington/Gower 1984).

Japan's Market, Michael Czinkota. A guide to the Japanese distribution system (Praeger 1986).

The Second Wave: Japan's Global Assault on Financial Services (Waterlow 1987).

Tokyo 200: The World's Third International Financial Centre, Economist Advisory Group (Economist Publications 1986).

Trojan Horse: The Ultimate Japanese Challenge to Western Industry, Barrie James (Mercury 1989).

EMPLOYMENT

How to Get a Job Abroad, Roger Jones (How To Books, 2nd edition 1991).

How to Teach Abroad, Roger Jones (How To Books, 1989).

Immigration: A Guide to Alien Procedures in Japan (Japan Times).

Japan Posting: Preparing to Live in Japan (British Chamber of Commerce in Japan 1990).

Jobs in Japan, J Wharton (Global Press/Vacation Work 1989).

Index

Addreses, coping with, 33, 120
Agriculture, 10
Ainu people, 10
Akihito, Emperor, 14
Alien registration, 31-32
American club, 80
American Occupation, 14, 71
Arashi, Mount, 11
Arriving in Japan, 25
Asahi newspaper, 122, 127

Babysitters, 81
Banking services, 30
Bathing, 80, 86
Berlitz, 47
Body language, 57, 60
Bonsai, 106
Breakfasts, 106
Buddhism, 12, 50, 123
Burakumin people, 10-11
Bushido, 51
Business dealings, 63ff
Business services, 26, 28, 114, 121

Car rental, 29
Chambers of Commerce, 37, 86
Chiba, 85
Chinese influences, 12
Christianity, 13, 51
Children, 24
Chopsticks, 59
Climate, 11, 22
Clinics and hospitals, 87-89
Clothing, 21
Comics (manga), 111
Confucianism, 51, 66
Counselling services, 90

Credit cards, 30

Culture, 49ff
Currency, 20, 29
Customs requirements, 20, 84

Dental care, 89
Domestic help, 81-82
Drama, 108-109
Drinks (alcoholic), 59-60, 73, 82-83, 105
Drinking water, 86
Driving, 100ff
Duty free shopping, 30

Eating, 59-60, 103ff
Economy of Japan, 15-18
Edo (Tokyo), 13
Education system, 92ff
Electricity, 81
Emergency services, 89-90
English language, 56
Entertaining, 72-74
Etiquette, 58-59

Festivals, 113
Food, 82, 103ff
Foreign Residents Advisory Centres, 85
Fukuoka, 25, 95
Furnishings, 80

Geography, 9
Gifts, giving of, 60, 74
Ginza shopping area, 121
GNP, 17
Go (board game), 109
Golf, 110-111
Government of Japan, 11ff

Great Depression, 13
Group ethos, 53

Handicrafts, 123-125
Haneda Airport, 25, 26
Health care, 86ff
Health insurance, 37, 90
Health regulations, 20
Hidyoshi Toyotomi, 12
Hiragana, 43
Hirohito, Emperor, 14
Hiroshima, 95
History, outline of Japanese, 11ff
Hokkaido, 9, 115
Holidays, 75
Honshu, 9
Hotels, 76-77, 115
Hours of work, 75
Housing, 78ff, 120

Ikebana, 107
Immigration, 19-20, 31-32
Income tax, 30-31
Industrial tours, 121, 130
Insurance, 36-37
International schools, 94ff
Interpreters, 72
Itami Airport, 25, 127

Japan Grey Line (bus services), 114
JapanRail Pass, 28, 116
Japan Travel-phone service, 121, 125, 130
Japanese Business Hotels Association, 77
JETRO (Japanese External Trade
    Organisation), 21
Jinmu, Emperor, 12
JNTO (Japan National Tourist
    Organisation), 137
JTB (Japan Travel Bureau), 115, 126,
    131
Judo, 112

Kabuki theatre, 108
Kamakura, 114
Kanagawa, 85
Kanji, 43
Kansai (central) area, 126
Karate, 110, 112-113
Katakana, 43

Kimonos, 22
Kobe, 95, 131-132
Korea, 10, 12
Kyoto, 96, 114-115, 122-126
Kyushu, 9, 11, 115

Language, Japanese, 41ff, 56, 72
Language schools, 46
Legal system, 71
Linguarama, 48
Literacy rate, 92
'Living National Treasures', 109
Loyalty at work, 66

Mah-jongg, 110
Marunouchi, 121
Meiji, emperor, 13, 15
Music, 108

Nagasaki, 13
Nagoya, 96
Nara, 115, 127
Narita Airport, 25
National Foundation Day, 12
Newspapers, 35-36
Night life, 73
Nikko, 114
Nissan Motor Company, 122
Noh theatre, 108

Okinawa, 98
Opera, 109
Origami, 108
Osaka, 12, 26, 28, 113, 126-132

Periodicals, 35-36
Perry, Commodore, 13
Pets, 31
Pharmacies, 90-91
Police services, 37, 90
Politics, 14
Pollution, 114
Population, 9ff
Postal services, 34-35
Public transport, 26

Radio broadcasting, 36
'Recruit scandal', 14
Religion, 9, 50ff

Rokko Mountains, 131-132
Ryokan (inns), 115

Sake, 105
Samurai, 12, 15, 51
Sapporo, 98
Sanitation, 80
Schools, 92ff
Shibuya, 121
Shikoku, 9
Shinjuku, 121
Shinkansen (high speed train), 27
Shinto religion, 9, 50ff, 123
Shoguns, 13
Shopping, 82ff, 121
Showa Era, 14
Shrines, 50, 123
Sports, 110ff
Status in Japanese life, 54
Stock Exchange, Tokyo, 122
Subway trains, 26, 121
Sukiyaki, 104
Sumo wrestling, 11-112
Suntory Brewery, 122
Sushi, 105

Taxation in Japan, 30-31
Taxis, 25, 28, 121
Tea ceremony, 60

Telecommunications, 33-34, 81
Television services, 36
Teyasu Tokygawa, 13
Tennis, 113
Theatre, 108-109
Tipping, 30
Tobacco, 82
Tokyo, 11, 25, 85, 96, 117-122
Tokyo Weekender, 80, 116
Toshiba Science Institute, 122
Tourist information services, 40, 125, 131, 130
Toyota Motor Corporation, 122
Trading companies ('shosha'), 16
Train services, 27

Universities, 93

Visas, 19, 31-32

Wa (harmony), 52-53, 68
War lords, 12
Women at work, 68-69, 84-85

Yayoi period, 12
Yokohama, 86, 98

Zen, 51, 107
Zoo, 127

How to Get a Job Abroad
Roger Jones BA (Hons) DipEd DPA

This great value-for-money paperback guide is essential reading for everyone planning to spend a period abroad. A key feature is the lengthy reference section of medium and long-term job opportunities and possibilities, arranged by region and country of the world, and by profession/occupation. There are more than 130 pages of specific contacts and leads, giving literally hundreds of addresses and much hard-to-find information. There is a classified guide to overseas recruitment agencies, and even a multi-lingual guide to writing application letters. The first edition of this popular handbook was published in 1989, and has since sold many thousands of copies. The book is now available in a second edition: it contains many new addresses and entries, and reflects recent political developments in Europe, the Gulf, and other parts of the world.

'A fine book for anyone considering even a temporary overseas job.' *The Evening Star.* 'A highly informative and well researched book . . . containing lots of hard information and a first class reference section . . . A superb buy.' *The Escape Committee Newsletter.* Roger Jones BA AKC DipTESL DipEd MInstAm DPA MBIM has himself worked abroad for many years in such varied locations as Austria, Cambodia, Thailand, Turkey and the Middle East. A specialist writer on expatriate and employment matters, he is also author of **How to Teach Abroad** in the same series.

288pp illustrated paperback. 1 85703 003 6. Second Edition

How to Study Abroad
Teresa Tinsley BA DipEd

Studying abroad can open up a whole new horizon of opportunities, but what courses are available? How does one qualify? What does it cost? Can anyone do it? This handy book brings together a wealth of fascinating advice and reference information for everyone who has dreamed of pursuing a course of studies abroad, from art and archaeology to languages, music, science and technology. Contents: why study abroad?, where to study?, what to study (everything from short study visits to postgraduate opportunities), getting a place, entrance requirements, when and how to apply, grants and scholarships, helpful agencies and contacts, validation of courses, fitting in, travel and visas, health and insurance. Complete with detailed country-by-country information. *160pp illustrated paperback. 07463 0340 8.*

How to Teach Abroad
Roger Jones BA(Hons) DipEd DPA

The complete guide to international opportunities and contacts.

> 'An excellent book . . . An exhaustive and practical coverage of the possibilities and practicalities of teaching overseas.' *The Escape Committee Newsletter.*

176pp illustrated paperback. 0743 0551 6.

How to Live & Work in America
Steve Mills BA(Hons) MA

America today is the number one destination for British and other expatriates. This highly readable and informative handbook explains America's rules and regulations on immigration: a jungle of quotas, green cards and special categories, plus work and lifestyle prospects in this ultimate land of opportunity. Steve Mills lectures at the University of Keele Centre for American Studies and has worked extensively in America.

> 'A mine of information.' *The Expatriate.*

244pp illustrated paperback. 1 85703 058 3. Second Edition.

How to Live & Work in Australia
Laura Veltman *Second edition*

The *Sydney-Sun-Herald* reported a massive 1,400 telephone calls a day to Australia House in London from would-be immigrants from Britain, with queues of personal callers stretching round the block. Never has there been such competition to get in. If *you* are competing for a place, *you* need **How to Live & Work in Australia,** packed from cover to cover with vital current information on costs, the crucial 'points' system, job opportunities, essential addresses, and domestic living in Australia today.

> 'One marvellous book. . . has just been published. . . it's written by Australian journalist Laura Veltman and she should know what she's talking about as she specialises in Australian migrant affairs. Written in a clear and entertaining style it provides all sorts of information (and) there's great good humour as Laura takes an honest look at Australian attitudes.' *Resident Abroad magazine.* 'Of interest to young travellers, too.' *The Times.* 'There has never been a better time to get hold of **How to Live & Work in Australia.'** *Southern X.*

244pp illustrated paperback. 1 85703 057 5. Second Edition.

How to Live & Work in Belgium
Marvina Shilling

Researched and written by a specialist on Belgian affairs, this is a complete manual of essential information on Belgium from entering the country to taking up residence, coping with the language, living in Brussels, Antwerp and other major cities, understanding the business, official and legal environment, the cost of living and other vital facts and advice for executives, officials, technicians, students, teachers and others.
128pp illustrated paperback. 0 7463 0564 8.

How to Live & Work in France
Nicole Prevost Logan

This book meets the need for a clear compendium of information and advice for longer-stay visitors or residents, whether their interests are commercial, official, technical, educational or lifestyle/retirement. It includes an extensive contacts section covering embassies and consulates, travel contacts, business contacts (including banks) in both Britain and France, and miscellaneous key addresses. Nicole Prevost Logan became licensed in Law at the University of Paris and obtained the Diploma in Political Science from the Institut D'Etudes Politiques. An experienced teacher, cultural adviser and student counsellor, she presently teaches French language and civilisation.

'A welcome addition to the list.' *Franco-British Society Newsletter.*

160pp illustrated paperback. 0 7463 05168.

How to Live & Work in Germany
Nessa Loewenthal

This is an exciting time to live in Germany. Whether you are planning to relocate for three months or three years, this is the book for you. It covers such practical topics as entry requirements, transportation, money matters, housing, schools, insurance and much besides. It also includes valuable pointers to German values, customs, business practices and etiquette to help you make the most of your stay. Nessa Loewenthal is Director of Trans Cultural Services, and a consultant specialising in intercultural briefing.
144pp, illustrated paperback. 185703 006 0.

How to Live & Work in Hong Kong
Martin Bennett

Hong Kong is one of the most dynamic centres in the world, and despite the shadow now hanging over its future, it remains an important centre for expatriates. This book will be essential reading for all business and professional people and their families planning to spend some time in Hong Kong. Authoritative and very comprehensive, it contains everything you need to know from the colony and its future to visas, permits and ID cards, money matters, crime and drugs, the Chinese way of business, festivals, being host or guest, social nuances, and a vast amount of other information.
144pp illustrated paperback. 1 85703 005 2.

How to Live & Work in Saudi Arabia
Margaret Nydell & Joy McGregor

In the wake of the Gulf war Saudi Arabia continues to offer well paid jobs for a whole range of expatriates from petroleum engineers to construction workers, and accountants to doctors, nurses and teachers. The book covers essential practical topics such as entry requirements, transport, money matters, housing, schools and insurance, plus vital pointers to Saudi Arabian values, customs, business practices and etiquette, providing a complete resource whether you are planning a stay of three months or three years. The authors have both lived and worked in Saudi Arabia for several years. Margaret Nydell teaches Arabic and is also author of *Understanding Arabs*.

> 'Commendably well written and achieves an unusually high level of accuracy of information . . . Balanced and shrewd.' *Middle East Association Information Digest.*

176pp illustrated paperback. 1 85703 007 9.

How to Live & Work in Spain
Robert A C Richards

Written by a British expatriate who has lived and worked in spain for more than 25 years, this new book provides a user-friendly guide for everyone planning to live in Spain on a temporary or permanent basis, and whether for business, professional purposes, study, leisure or retirement. Written with gusto, the book gives a fascinating warts'n'all account of Spain's variegated lifestyles and how to cope.
160pp illustrated paperback. 1 85703 011 7.